The Historical Series of the Reformed Church in America

No. 10

"B. D."

A Biography of my Father, the Late Reverend B. D. Dykstra

by

D. IVAN DYKSTRA

Wm. B. Eerdmans Publishing Co.
Grand Rapids, Michigan

Library of Congress Cataloging in Publication Data

Dykstra, D. Ivan.
  "B.D." : a biography of my father, the late Reverend B.D. Dykstra.

  (The Historical series of the Reformed Church in America; no. 10)
    1. Dykstra, B. D. 2. Reformed Church—Clergy—Biography. 3. Clergy—United States—Biography.
  I. Title. II. Series.
  BX9593.D94D94 1982   285.7'32'0924 [B]   82-8737
  ISBN 0-8028-1945-1   AACR2

To Katy

*The relation of mutual respect and affection
between her and my father has
heightened my perception of both.*

The Historical Series of the Reformed Church in America

This series has been inaugurated by the General Synod of the Reformed Church in America, acting through its Commission on History, for the purpose of encouraging historical research and providing a medium wherein this knowledge may be shared with the academic community and with the members of the denomination in order that a knowledge of the past may contribute to right action in the present.

Editor

The Rev. Donald J. Bruggink, Ph.D., Western Theological Seminary

The Commission on History

The Rev. Arie R. Brouwer, D.D., General Secretary, R.C.A.
The Rev. Elton J. Bruins, Ph.D., Hope College
Professor Gerald F. De Jong, Ph.D., University of South Dakota
Professor Barbara Walvoord, Ph.D., Loyola College of Maryland
Barbara Frierson, Oakland, California
The Rev. Norman J. Kansfield, Ph.D., Western Theological Seminary
The Rev. Joseph A. Loux, Jr., Helderberg Reformed Church, Guilderland Center, New York

Contents

		Page
	Prologue	1
I	Roots	7
II	A New Land	17
III	Education	29
IV	The Golden Age	42
V	Variations On A Theme	64
VI	God's Greyhound	78
VII	Marriage and The Family	91
VIII	Pacifism	104
IX	The Editor's Chair	121
X	The Man On A Bicycle	139

Acknowledgement

This is a biography of *my* father. But he was the father of others, too. What they are makes up a very large part of the substance of his personal eminence. Hence this expression of my appreciation
   to my sisters:
      Betsche Kenno (Betty)—Mrs. Marion Schippers.
      Avah Talitha (Ava)—Mrs. Dwight Berkebile
   and to my brothers:
      Adelphos Antonius (deceased)
      Anthony Pacifer
      Clemens Aquila (deceased)
      Reinard Hessel
      Wesley Calvin
      Vergil Homer
      Emanuel David

PROLOGUE

I do confess, as I offer this biography of my father, to a little twinge of anxiety. There is a certain natural image associated with a biography. It is that its subject must be deserving of it, either by virtue of his having had a publicly significant career, as evidenced by distinguished positions held or special honors won, or by virtue of his being generally interesting to at least a reasonably significant number of persons. In the absence of either of those, a biography too easily slides over into being a promotional sheet which is designed either to magnify the overt accomplishments or to create an interest.

Such anxieties over a possible presumptiveness in writing a biography would be more telling were this to be an autobiography. But as a biography it is, after all, about *my* father. And though I write it out of a deep and abiding affection and admiration for him for which I need make no apology, it is a delicate task to magnify *his* significance without letting this be done from self-interest.

The proper response to this image of a biography having to be, in the sense mentioned, deserved is that really it is not the publicly recognized significance of the subject's achievement that qualifies him or anyone else for a biographical treatment. The real qualification must consist rather in this, that particular people are simply inherently interesting. When one considers that, any fear of presumptiveness in writing a biography gives way to a feeling of loss because we do not do much, much more of it. By that standard of being inherently interesting, I could without trying very hard think of a great many people who would be deserving of biographical treatment. In fact, it would be much harder to think of anyone, whatever his or her station in life, who would not qualify as fit subject of biographical study. Fortunately, the current surge of interest in "oral history" is a good move toward recognizing this.

But if in undertaking to do a biography one does experience that anxiety, at the end it is easily forgotten in the rich experience of doing a biography. Almost any articulation of anything at all is a meaningful process of self-discovery as much as it is a discovery of something else or of another. There are many available ways of discovering or defining oneself, but among them this must rank high, that we discover and define ourselves by our reactions, pro or con, to other persons. Since this is to be a biography of my father, this self-discovery could easily become a matter of self-discovery by finding my "roots" in the life of my father. And some of that does find its way into the following pages. But it is a gross over-simplification to imagine that the relation of father to son is simply a relation of cause and effect. Persons are, after all, much too complicated to be caught up in the "inheritance" image, whether it be genetic, psychological, or cultural. It is much more meaningful, consequently, to let the image of self-discovery center less on the notion of inheritance and more on the image of interaction, or action and reaction.

What, along with his being interesting for his own sake, makes my father a fit subject for a biography is that he was, probably more than any other person I have known, a completely reflective and articulate person. Particularly during the span of years when he served as a newspaper editor did he leave a readily accessible record of his reflections. But that covered the relatively short span of eight or nine years of his life. Beyond that, however, he was simply a tireless writer. His trusty, usually scratchy dip-pen was certainly as intergral a part of him as the fingers of his hand. Especially during his years as an editor he must have spent as much as up to sixty hours a week writing. And during those years he expressed his gratitude that he had the help of having to meet deadlines. These forced him to put pen to paper even when he did not feel directly inspired to write, and saved him from the damaging luxury of feeling he had to think everything through in completely finished form before beginning to write. The writing process, he discovered, was itself the act of discovery and not just the act of transcribing what had been discovered.

But outside the years as editor, the writing was no less incessant, though from the extant papers it is clear that then his favorite literary style was that of poetry—and the sermon. But the sermons were, with only a couple of exceptions, not written. All that is left of them is a series of topics and subtitles on which to hang his oral reflections. And most of these were written on the clean side of postal envelopes that had been slit open.

The writing, as one would expect particularly during the years as editor, was about a very great variety of matters, some about events of current interest, others about matters of more perennial interest. But he also did a very great deal of writing about himself. He was, as he said, interested in everything that had anything to do with being a human being alive in the world. He made his own the line from the German poet, which in his Dutch read, "Niets menschelijks is mij vreemd" (Nothing that belongs to being human is a matter of indifference to me). I would find it quite impossible to answer the question whether he was more interested in writing about what was going on around him "out there," or about himself. If I were forced to answer, I could only tilt toward the latter and judge that, more clearly than he may himself have realized, his writing and reflecting were primarily a matter of his inner pilgrimage, or, to borrow the title of the memoirs of Pope John XXIII, "the autobiography of a soul."

But his unplanned and spontaneous and uncalculating interest in understanding himself showed as much in many things he said, as if in passing, as in what he wrote. An often-repeated phrase ran: "If you want to understand me, you must begin with . . ."; and without having to try very hard I can recall quite a variety of completions for the statement.

The survival, now in writing, of that many of his own direct appraisals of himself and his life could, it is true, call in question the propriety of doing a biography at all. Why do a biography when there exists what amounts really to an autogiobraphy? The response to that has to call up the image of a kind of paradox involved in trying to relive another person's life. There surely can be no argument about the fact that any person has to be respected as the final authority on what he is. Only he could know, because only he could speak from inside himself, what he was. Still that is not the last word, by so much as one who talks about himself lives too close to himself to be able to have an assured clear perspective on what he is. And it is the latter consideration that warrants a biography, to go along with the autobiography.

The comments above must leave the impression that my father, in so far as a general public recognition of his character and achievements is concerned, did live obscurely. In a way, he can be described as a nobody. Of him, some said, "he threw his life away," presumably on little insignificant nothings. And he did think of himself as not really having "amounted to very much," while being honestly humble enough to have taken some pride in being able to say that.

But that is not the whole truth. Though it is correct to say that, as far as his ever having held a position that would bring him any kind of recognition is concerned, he was an obscure figure, it is equally correct to say that anyone who knew him or of him was pretty likely to be vividly aware of him. He was indeed a presence to be reckoned with, in a way in which I hope this biography can make clear. As one small underscoring of that fact, I mention one little phenomenon which as much as anything pushed my long-standing desire to do a biography of my father toward this fruition. This past summer his family met for one of its rare reunions. And one had to stand in awe of the fact that during those days together no one talked at all about his or her own career. Virtually every conversation revolved around our father in some way—and that twenty-five years after his death. And for me, one of the bright experiences of my life is the remembrance of how many and how many widely different kinds of people from all walks of life have had some interesting and significant and appreciative thing to say about him. All of that, along with a great flood of personal memories and his own self-articulations, is what makes this biography possible.

I
"Roots"

My father was Dutch, a native of the Netherlands. And that fact is of major importance for understanding him. For all his life he was heavily influenced by an ethnic-consciousness which, however, had a very special meaning for him which our somewhat vague images of ethnicity do not quite capture.

But though after his family's emigration to America when he was eleven years old he was for the most part dominated by a strong sense of his identity as Dutch, in his earlier and formative years something else was much more important. It was the fact that, within the broader Dutch identity, he was Frisian.

The Netherlands as a whole is not a large country geographically, as nations go—roughly the size of our state of Maryland. It is hard for us, even against the background of our self-characterization as "the melting pot" of many nationalities, to appreciate either the cultural diversity that could occupy so small an area, or the extent to which these had, at least up to his time, resisted the kind of amalgamation that the term "melting pot" suggests. Holland is divided into eleven provinces, but the provincial divisions are in no way artificially drawn or dictated by the accidents of geography or politics. They are rather the result of very old tribal identities, and Holland is primarily a kind of political umbrella which arches over these separate tribal identities.

Fortunately for us, among the papers he left behind there is a memoir of some twenty pages which is his retrospective on his years in the Netherlands. It is a beautiful literary piece, written in fictional-descriptive style, but fictional only to the extent that he appears in it as the small boy named "Friso." My father did now and then try his hand at a fictional literary style but it did not fool anybody. He was quite incapable of the kind of smooth invention which we properly associate with the writer of novels or stories. In even his efforts to be literary he was very much confined to factually actual circumstances; and when these were talked about in a more-than-the-bare-facts style, the feeling qualities were not loosely tacked on or read into the facts.

From that memoir about his life before he was eleven, it is clear that his sense of the cultural and temperamental distinctions within the Netherlands was not something he had later learned from books, though it was confirmed by what he found later. This identification of how people from the different provinces differed from each other he became aware of even as a child listening to his elders' repetitions of existing folk-lore. And I remember something of that consciousness of provincial differences even from my own childhood. To the loose extent to which the Dutch immigrants to America tended to cluster here and there according to their provincial origins there was a vague cataloguing of community temperaments: this community was mainly from the Gelderland province so they were inclined to be sentimental; those over yonder from another province were hard-headed "men of affairs", et cetera. So it was with the Frisians. My father was not first of all conscious of his ethnicity in the sense that in this country he was Dutch, over against the "world out there." Even in Friesland (or Frisia, as he preferred to name it) the Frisians had a powerful sense of not really being identified with the larger Dutch entity. Though this would not be true of each of the Dutch provinces, despite their origins in different tribal identities, the Frisians have a culture and a language and a character of their own which from the days of the Roman Empire they have fought to preserve. Other provincial languages may be spoken of as Dutch dialects, but not the Frisian. Its clearer association is with the Anglo-Saxon, and some more ambitious Frisians, clearly not without some warrant, will make the claim that Frisia more than anything else is the cradle of Anglo-Saxon civilization.

So, far more important in the description of my father than that he was Dutch is the fact that he was Frisian. But what then marked off the Frisians from the others? The image is considerably different from at least our prevailing stereotypes of the Dutch.

From somewhere in the past I remember my father's remark: "If you want to understand me, you must begin with the fact that I was born on the shores of the North Sea and on the twenty-first of November." What that was supposed to point to in himself was his quality of austerity. This image, I think, is quite misleading, as a description of the Frisian temperament and also as a description of my father's boyhood experiences. I can only interpret the quotation as intending to be a father's apology in his later and mellower years for feeling that he had treated his family with a greater degree of austerity than he later wished he had.

It is not with austerity that a description of the Frisians (or of my father) must begin. If that is there, it is there only as a by-product of something else. They do better who put at the center the Frisians' love of liberty—but importantly not for themselves alone but for others. For what it is worth, this *is* symbolized in the interesting fact that the Frisians were the first political entity to formally recognize the independence of the American colonies. But even the phrase "love of liberty" does not quite catch the spirit. Rather call it the instinct for self-reliance—not to become either inhibited by or obligated to anyone or anything. And if there is anything else to add to this, the second belongs to the first in the way in which one side of a coin belongs to the other. It is the instinct for preserving one's identity. This fact puts into its proper perspective my father's enthusiastic endorsement of Emerson's classic "Essay on Self-Reliance."

But beyond that there are quite a few things this does not mean. The wish to preserve an identity does not become a conservative holding on to neat structuredness. This is apparent even in the difference between the Dutch and Frisian languages. Dutch is an elegant and elegantly structured language. A Frisian sentence simply seems to flow. And in reading a Frisian sentence I feel a certain anxiety about whether the sentence is going to include everything it needs to make sense, with afterwards a little feeling of surprise that all the elements did get into the picture plus a few others. A Frisian simply does not "play it safe," or if he does seem now and then to play it close to the vest it is only so that he does not, by overextending himself, get trapped into a situation where he is at the mercy of something beyond his control.

In respect to the love of liberty, for others as well as for oneself or for one's own, the Frisian temperament walks the fine line between a skepticism about the merit of any culture (which is the mishmash of convictionless indifference) and a sectarian writing off of anything that differs from ours as being of the devil. My father did, as I shall point out, have his times when he felt that "the world out there" was an evil which threatened to undo him, but that had a very different inspiration.

Much of the Frisian instinct for self-reliance we read from the Frisians' epic reclamation of land from the Zuider Zee. There is probably nothing in history that can quite match that achievement or even the conception of it. Among all the things it has to say is that the Frisians were committed to making it, but not at someone else's expense—as by military conquest of one's neighbor's lands. The ultimate competition was not between them and others but between them and their circumstances. And the Zuider Zee conquest stands not only as a monument to their industriousness, but as a correct index to their character; not for them the pallid heroism of whipping themselves into an abject acceptance of their lot in life—only the heroism of tackling the impossible and doing it themselves.

This passion for self-reliance, so nearly uniquely expressed in terms of a life of gusto, was not merely confined to being a characteristic of a group as over against another group. It carried over into a self-reliance of each individual over against other individuals. Whatever meaning the phrase "rugged individualism" has acquired in our American consciousness, it has a possibly even stronger temperamental connotation for the Frisian. One of the interesting revelations I have had only belatedly, as a result of examining my father's literary remains, is the extent to which his positions on many issues simply seem to have been shaped by this self-reliance instinct, though the subject-matters are very, very diverse and though the particular idioms for its expression vary wonderfully.

As for my father's account in the memoir on his childhood years in Friesland, everything in it belies the hint that it was a life of austerity. In every respect he remembered it as being indeed truly idyllic. It was pastoral, but dynamic; peaceful, but humming. It was not that nothing disadvantageous ever occurred. With his family's home but two miles inland from the sea shore and the land well below sea-level, winter's storms did hold their terrors and wreak their havoc. But events such as those were, for the Frisian, filtered through his temperamental lenses which saw them not as if visitations of an angry God but as challenges to get back to work.

My father speaks of wandering along the dikes with his playmates, or wandering off alone picking wild flowers. Two things he remembered especially, the sight of the cattle in the "polders" (Friesland has recently been described as the only country in the world where cattle outnumber the people) and the ships sailing out to sea (a special sight in Friesland where the ships move through the canals which run through the countryside but eerily above the level of the land alongside the canals). But though, and probably more in retrospect than at the time, the moving ships did contain a hint of and beckoned to the large, large world that lay beyond, the clearer attention was on the nearer at hand living cattle—a preview of what was to be one important feature of his subsequent experience.

Despite a long-standing family mythology which has always imagined my father's childhood as having been spent in poverty, this certainly was not the case, at least during the years in Friesland. Information about the family's circumstances is scant, but such clues as there are have to point to a life even of some affluence. An autobiographical statement written within a year of his death informs us for the first time that the family owned "four hundred units of land", and a "unit" was roughly three-fourths of an acre. Thus his family was, by European standards, reasonably well landed, if not by the standards of our western ranches or of the modern agribusiness domains of the midwest, then certainly by the standards of the Iowa and South Dakota which we knew in our childhood. My father speaks of the farm laborers imported from Ost-Friesland in northwest Germany as they swung their scythes rhythmically in the harvest fields. One of my brothers shares an interesting little confirmation of this well-being, Not having inherited his father's passion for rising promptly and early in the morning, my father would on occasion chide him with, "Just like your grandfather—always wanting to stay in bed until noon." With virtually nothing else to go on about my grandfather, that little glimpse is enough to suggest that he was, or at least thought of himself as being, a member of the landed gentry and thus above manual labor. This is reinforced by the reference to his mother as having had "the good fortune to attract the attention and win the affection of a widowed landowner, some years older". My father speaks, in his memoir on Friesland, about how the landed estates lay interspersed among the homes of the poor, and of how he never felt any discomfort about mingling with the children from among the poor and humble workers—which one would not say if he were himself poor and humble. And he speaks with a special awe of a Samson-like "big Wytse", who during the recesses between his regular stints in the local jail for what was probably his drunken brawling in the streets, was employed solely to shine up the cows' horns, during which he also held the neighborhood children enthralled with his story-telling. All of that points to a life of considerable affluence—to the extent that it is hard to harmonize that picture with anything else we were to see in my father later.

And then there was school, about which the memoir goes into delightful detail. Until the discovery of the memoir there was always some puzzlement on our part over how it came about that my father, whom we thought of as a "farm boy from Iowa" and for whom taking career-initiatives was not a strong point, could have gotten to the point of breaking out of his farm background to go "away to college" (which happened rarely at the turn of the century in Iowa) and finally even got into the educational big time by spending a year at Yale. That mystery is dissipated in large part by the knowledge that education played an exceptionally large role among the Frisians and its importance loomed large in their natural consciousness. (Even now, by one report, over half the faculties in the Dutch universities are native Frisians).

Interestingly, and probably significantly, while the memoir goes into great detail about life in school, there is simply no reference either to church or to piety. Well, there is one. It makes mention only, while describing the delights and the exceptional functionality of the wooden shoe, of the fact that there were always special "Sunday" wooden shoes, painted black with white-flowered designs. It is hard to doubt that there was some piety involved, but if so I should judge that it was not a particularly self-conscious piety but rather more nearly like a strand subconsciously woven into the fabric of the community folk-lore. All later family mythology about a background of piety revolves only around my father's mother, who (as was, I think, not uncommon even among the Dutch in this country) appears to have been much more the bearer of piety than was my grandfather.

A few more wisps reinforce this image of an early family life not particularly dominated by piety. Of three of the four of my father's sisters whom we got to know, two were simply indentified as "humanists," and the third, though outstandingly active in churchly affairs and the promotion of good causes, had a prominent streak of what at least loosely could be called "humanism." She was a beautifully and sensitively articulate person, but her articulations seemed to betray a personal ideology that drew its inspirations much more from the great literary classics than from more specifically religious sources like the Bible or the classic literature of devotion. Of the visits by the unabashedly "humanist" aunts I do have a clear recollection, especially when one of them stuck vigorously with her kind of agnosticism even as her end neared. They certainly were identified as something different from the overwhelming majority of the people we knew, and while there may have been a little feeling on our part that they were a little odd, mostly there were some barely suppressed instincts that held them in special awe. And given the powerful and omnipresent religiousness of the community in which they and my father lived, even that was more interesting because it was accompanied with a rather definite feeling of naughtiness in our privately holding them in special esteem.

What gives that bit its importance for my father's biography is that it may explain, and enable me to go on to, something quite precise about his religiousness. That he was in every visible way heavily into religion and theology is certainly true. Much of what he talked and wrote about was overtly theological in substance, and even when the subject-matters were not specifically theological, theological considerations kept appearing in how he handled them. And there simply can be no arguing with what he said of himself in the last *Apologia* which he wrote shortly before he died: "I have tried above everything to be a faithful servant of Jesus Christ." And there the matter ought to rest.

But that does not by any means take everything into account. For one thing, my father certainly was not overawed by piety. Much of what he thought even religiously was in sharp criticism at least of the institutionalized forms of piety, but even in his piety he often stood alone against what piety was by common consent supposed to look like. In a community in which it was for a time nearly correct to say that whether one attended church twice on a Sunday was what finally distinguished the truly elect from the borderline elect, and while insisting that the family walk the mile and a half to church twice on a Sunday, he only on the rarest occasions would attend church twice. When it was considered a minor scandal to let children engage in a little innocent ball-playing on a Sunday afternoon, he encouraged us and even got himself involved in playing ball, right out in the open where the parade of home-going churchgoers could see us.

What that suggests is at least a picture of one who, though heavily involved in religious matters, did hold religiousness somewhat at arm's length. There were family devotions before and after each of the three meals a day, but it was not always clear whether what we got was simply religious devotion or the discoveries of great literature. Most impressively though he was professionally involved as an ordained clergyman and thus in the religious vocation, he acted in the capacity of a parish minister for only a relatively short span of nine years, and for some of that time he acted only as a week-end parson. From Monday morning to Friday night he was in academic work. And the same *Apologia* which contains the "good servant of Jesus Christ" passage also points to his having been, by a perhaps even more elemental instinct, a teacher and dominated by an incessant intellectual curiosity.

What this points to is at least the fact that rather than letting everything revolve around the single center of religiousness he was rather bipolar in his interests. His religiousness at least had to share the spotlight, in his sensitivities, with his intellectual and academic interests. But all of this and a few other cues besides this points to something else.

The dominant thing about my father, as what follows will make clear in many ways, is that he was so thoroughly an "inner-directed" or an inwardly determined person. Things "sprang from his nature," and a large part of his personal power (and part of his limitations) lay exactly in that. Everything had the ring of authenticity, integrity, genuiness. And in retrospect, but with much that points in that direction, that held for everything except his theological interests. Nor is it only in retrospect. I remember feeling tempted on a few occasions during my teens to ask him whether that interpretation would have been correct, though I never was able to muster the requisite courage to put the question to him.

What tends to confirm that is his own reference to how he got into the religious vocation in the first place. There was, it is true, the influence of his mother which gave him some predisposition toward such a calling. But what drove him into the religious vocation, I judge, was not some powerful inner drive or sense of calling. It came about more specifically by way of what seems to have been a fairly casual suggestion from some of his college teachers that he go this route. And the most persuasive suggestion came from one who was simply impressed by his speaking ability, which my father never realized until then he had. I have no doubt about this that he became as heavily involved as he did through most of his career in religious and theological concerns because he had thus become involved in the religious professionally, rather than that he got into the profession because of some powerful inner drive. If this needs further justification it is in the fact that all his life, and in a way sometimes plaintively, he seemed to want to be and thought he ought to be somewhere else—and that did not mean in the church. I think few things are more decisive in getting to an exactly correct understanding of my father than this.

But all of that has turned out to be a fairly long digression from the story of his first day in school. And that was something else! He has told of this in the memoir on his Friesland days, in great and intriguing detail. What happened was that somewhere during that day, possibly toward its close, the pupils were asked to turn in their slates to the teacher, and this father whom we would have expected in his childhood to be a completely decent and law-abiding little citizen simply refused. It is not clear why this happened. One would like to dramatize it as being an expression of the proverbial Frisian stubbornness; knowing how often later he was to describe himself as a very shy person, a more likely theory is that he simply panicked, or saw only that something was being taken away from him which he might not get back. At any rate he refused.

Well! that kind of challenge to authority was not likely to go unchallenged anywhere and even less so in Friesland, where a hefty temper seemed to belong with nature's other endowments. So out came the teacher's rod, all eight feet of it, long enough to reach the pupil in the middle of the long rows of desks. But my father was not finished; he grabbed the descending rod, not knowing that its center had already been secretly weakened by an earlier prankster, and he quite easily broke it in two. And for that he was picked up bodily and flung into the peat-bin (the equivalent of our later coal-bin).

Nor did the matter rest there. The little war between teacher and pupil must have created something of a sensation. At any rate it was followed by what appears to have been roughly the equivalent of a formal hearing before the membership of the Parent Teachers Association, during which the teacher reportedly declared "I would have killed him!"

I have wondered since whether the memory of that terrifying introduction to school had anything to do with how my father later, when he was himself the schoolmaster, would handle at least the minor unrests that seem to be endemic to classrooms the world over. For him then no eight foot rods or casting into coal-bin dungeons. Instead, when attention wavered or tittering began, he simply put down his book, took off his spectacles and solemnly announced, "We will have five minutes of silence"—or it might be ten, depending on the sense of how large the interruptions threatened to become. And do not think we were getting off scot-free. Those silences simply dripped damnations all over the place; any of us would, I think, gladly have accepted a sharp rap or two from the rod and had done with it, rather than endure the unending agony of having to live for five minutes in public with our own sense of abject shame. But in many ways throughout his life, his effect on the people with whom he came in contact showed something of that. It was at the same time the secret of the power of his presence and made him difficult to cope with, other than by an inner or outer temperamental lashing back.

The sequel to what must have been that very traumatic first day in school was a much happier one than would have been believed possible. The teacher, whether from remorse or from a fear perhaps of losing his position, or simply because he saw something in my father that he had not been able to see that first day, simply did a complete about-face toward him. My father appears to have been a very diligent and capable pupil who thoroughly enjoyed his schooling and the fact is that he was on many occasions over the years singled out for his excellence in his studies and explicitly acknowledged before visitors to have been the school's model pupil—which I suppose did not exactly endear him to his peers.

If such recognition was not the cause of, then it can only have greatly abetted my father's feeling about himself that he was a very special person, not only in his own eyes but in the eyes of other persons. From those early school days on he thought of himself as different, even set apart. To say that he had a kind of messianic self-consciousness would be putting the matter too strongly, but there was at least a little touch of that. And that feeling was abetted by his discovery some years later that at the age of around two, his family's homestead had burned to the ground and for a time he had been thought to have been lost in the flames. But unknown to the family, a neighbor lady had removed him from the house and carried him a safe distance away and deposited him in a grainfield. This my father saw as being not wholly without analogy to the ancient Moses, for whom his fortuitous rescue from a death he should have shared with the other Hebrews babies had all the force of a "wonder-birth" which marked him off as special. I can easily imagine my father making that comparison. It would surely be a mistake to interpret that in too solemn a manner. He had a poet's free-roaming instinct for seeing connections and analogies everywhere, but he might have told of this one with a gentle twinkle in his eye. But however lightly, the idea did occur to him and he fancied it. And what I have referred to with the only term that captures the feeling, of being set apart and special in a manner such that only the term "messianic self-consciousness" can do it justice even though it must be only mildly applied, I now judge was a very major clue in understanding my father. He simply was never able to think of himself as an ordinary mortal among mortals.

Since to those who knew him in a general way, he appeared always as a very humble and self-effacing person, one would expect that the sense of being special might be read to mean a fundamental humility. If specially called, that had to mean called to perform some special mission in life. And I can find much that points to that. But the sense of being special was not always confined to its humbler meanings; it was not always free of a trace of pride of self and of the expectation that as a person set apart life would also hold some special bonuses for him. More positively, that sense of specialness was over the years to weave itself into a design of many varying episodes. It is hard to convey adequately how fateful this sense of being specially set apart was for the future shape of his career, and particularly for what he for a time late in life sensed to be deeply the pathos of his career. The feeling of being special I suppose strikes one as being all gain. In my father's case many of its consequences were negative.

But the Frisian idyll was to come to an end. In 1882, when my father was in his eleventh year, the family made the great decision to emigrate to America. And my father's last recollection of the homeland he was never to see again was that of the family trudging together to the city of Harlingen, not far distant. But what he remembered most vividly about that was that he walked that day hand in hand with the very schoolmaster of the slate and cudgel fame. And as they turned away to board their ship for America, the schoolmaster for yet one more time exhorted my father's parents above all to assure that, once landed in America, they would make possible for my father the kind of education that would be worthy of his talents.

This, it is clear in retrospect, made a great and lasting impression on him, coming as it did on top of some years of applause for his academic achievements and promise. I suppose that what we like best to think about ourselves is that we become what we become in life as a consequence of our having caught hold of some clear purpose, which we then steadfastly pursue to fruition. This can happen and does, but certainly not always and perhaps not often. As often we are shaped, quite subconsciously, by our lurking self-images. And these are in turn shaped by what someone at an opporture time may have said to or about us, even if it is said in passing or by way of random exploration of what our possibilities may be or while fumbling for some appropriate thing to say on the occasion of a farewell. This is particularly so if what is said is laudatory and if the one of whom it is said is inclined to be shy and unsure. And if it is true that "there is destiny that shapes our ways, rough-hew them though we may," the angels of that destiny may well be such a casual remark.

And so the curtain fell for my father on Friesland. In America a whole new chapter would begin. But Friesland was not wholly put aside. From his earliest years after his formal education was completed, the extant papers indicate that my father's literary output was almost wholly in poetic form. But of what is left, the poetry seems to be roughly equally divided between English, Dutch, and Frisian. In that way he kept the Frisian spirit alive in himself.

And there was a sequel. Sixty years after emigrating, after his connection as editor had terminated and everything seemed to be in hiatus, virtually as a hobby he turned back to his Frisian heritage. This may have been with some feeling of turning back to his roots at a time when life seemed aimless. But the dimensions of that grew into a zest for promotion of the Frisian language and culture, and he threw himself into this with a great deal of satisfaction. In Iowa he was instrumental in the establishment of a Frisian society *Us Heiteloan*, and he developed a lively and for him vitally important contact with an existing Frisian society in Grand Rapids. This major involvement in Grand Rapids came in the form of his development of a formal church worship service done wholly in Frisian. The marvel about that, as I remember, was that it was so novel; one would have imagined that it would have been commonplace. Preparation included not only writing the sermon but preparing translations of "gospel hymns" into Frisian, and so on. Those Frisian services proved to be a heady experience, not only because by this he could drink once more at the old fountains but because the services "packed the people in."

I am not sure I can vouch wholly for the factual accuracy of the following, but I can vouch at least for the fact that this is how the family's mythology got to interpret it. In his renewed interest in the Frisian culture he also discovered that there was an existing Frisian society in California as well, I believe in San Francisco. But this was something quite different from what he had found in Grand Rapids, or than he had founded in Iowa. In the latter two areas the Frisians were reasonably devout and church-going people, and a natural interest around which to rally them could be the religious service.

But Frisians are by no means always that devout. If they could produce a virile piety they could also produce a pretty virile secularism—free-thinking, hard-drinking. Such, by the mythology's impression, were the San Francisco Frisians. And for them no church service would do, even if it were in the language of the fatherland. But my father was not daunted—nor foolish. He had discovered a Frisian language version of our old English classic, Tennyson's *Enoch Arden*, which he memorized. It became a recitation that went on for a good hour and a half. *This*, he supposed, could play in San Francisco even if Jesus Christ could not—and it did. How could it miss? All the ingredients were there—a saga of the sea for a one-time fisherman people, powerful romance, and all delivered up in the language of the fatherland. They obviously loved it!

II
"A New Land"

By the available information, which is scant but clear, as to the reasons for the emigration, they were mainly economic. For a good deal of the nineteenth century Dutch emigration to America religious factors were at least present, though it is hard to say just how influential they may have been in comparison with the economic. Some of the information has been filtered through a Dutch-American folklore which sought to underscore and perpetuate the image of Dutch piety. There were few more effective ways of doing this than to make much of the fact that it was the wish to preserve their religious convictions intact in the face of religious persecution which more than anything else prompted the exodus. That image is underscored by the fact that in at least some instances in the immigration into western Michigan the migrants came to this country under the leadership of their clergy, who simply brought their congregations over with them. One notable example of this was the settlement of Holland, Michigan, under the leadership of the Reverend Albertus C. Van Raalte in 1847. Lesser known is the fact that Van Raalte, a person of obviously many-sided genius, by no means envisioned that Holland would provide primarily a safe haven for his persecuted people. Equally he envisioned his project in ambitious economic terms, with some vision of Holland as the industrial hub for which the surrounding settlements would provide the materials. This image is more consistent with, in a broad and long historical perspective, the Dutch character. Though long on religious convictions, they did not interpret this typically in terms of a placid folded-hands kind of piety. The Calvinistic piety either produced or was not an interference with a civilization that was vigorous and aggressive in both industry and trade. The Dutch had developed one of the great empires, and at least by their founding of New York, at one time could easily have been conceived of as coming to exercise the dominant role in the new world which was actually played by the British Empire.

In so far as it would be correct to speak of religious persecution, it occurred in the context of the tension between the "state church" and the "free churches." And the latter phrase easily slips out of focus and comes to have quite different connotations than it had originally, as intending simply the independence of the church institution from state control or management. The Protestant Reformation had achieved the independence of the churches from Rome, but Roman authority was simply replaced by the authority of national churches, in Holland as in Germany and England, for but a few examples. In each case, the national church was not separate from the government. In the Netherlands the government did assume a large measure of control over religious affairs, though it is not clear at the beginning whether this involved more than just a commitment to sponsor that good cultural thing which we call religion. Eventually the Reformed Churches emerged as the state church. To examine the large issue of just what forces lay behind this, or the equally large issue of what forces prompted dissent from such an arrangement, would carry this too far afield. It is a complex matter to determine whether, for instance, the free churches simply objected in principle to the church's having to be under the jurisdiction of the state, or whether there were at stake certain specifically religious convictions which were being infringed on by the state. This historic conflict between the state church and the free churches formed an interesting backdrop for my father's later strong commitment to the belief that education should also not be a function of the state—nor of a church, for that matter; it was to be guarded jealously as exclusively the function of the home, and of such more ambitious educational arrangements as might be contrived by parents acting in conjunction with other parents in formal associations for the conduct of the schools.

The fact is that in speaking of the reasons for his family's emigration my father makes no references to there having been religious reasons. But he does speak explicitly of economic reasons. Even this should not, however, conjure up visions of anything like the Irish potato famines, which confronted the Irish with the stark choice, "Get out or starve!" But the trouble was real and the future looked even more grim. The Netherlands did feel the effects of the economic depression following the Franco-Prussian war. Land values had plunged by half. Not out of desperation but from foresight, my father's family sold its land before its values hit bottom, but obviously as yet with no serious thought about emigration. Only when alternative plans failed to materialize did the prospect of emigration loom larger.

This was made easier by the fact that one of his mother's two remaining brothers had, not from economic necessity but simply because of the lure of the new world, already emigrated to settle in northwest Iowa, so there was from him a flow of information about conditions there. The result was that in May of 1882 the family set sail for America, together with the family of her other brother, on the Holland-American Lines' *Schiedam*.

The family then comprised, along with the parents, seven children, of which my father was the fifth in line. First came two sisters, then two brothers, and when he came along his mother had decided that it was now time for another daughter but it turned out to be not so. The frequency with which I remember his mentioning that little circumstance suggests that it made some kind of special mark on his consciousness, even though his mother in the end could know that things had evened out, with four sons and four daughters. One son died in boyhood, another, next older to my father, died in his twenties, and one sister died somewhere before our time.

The only remarkable thing I can say about my father's father is that never in my life did I hear a reference of any kind made to him by my father. I am sure this is not a matter of my having forgotten such references. There simply were none. The tiny bits of information above I learned only from my father's papers. It would be too hasty to infer from this any particular estrangement from his father. There is a possible inference from my father's self-confessed shyness that he felt no easy bond with his landowner (and probably proud of it) father. It is safer to attribute this silence concerning his father simply to the age-spans that separated the generations. After all, when I was born my father was already forty-five. I have found no direct statement about the dates either of his father's birth or death. There is his reference in a note about life on the farm in Iowa to his father's having taken no active part in the work of the farm because of his age of sixty-six. If that means, as it plausibly does, that his father was sixty-six in the year of emigration, that would have put his birthdate in 1816.* And by a similarly indirect calculation about my father's mother's birthdate, that would have made him thirty years older than grandmother. It is also clear that his father died not too many years after the emigration, almost certainly no later than in 1890. Thus by the time I was old enough to hear about grandfathers, mine would have been pretty much a faded memory, especially if no real rapport had developed between father and son. I do remember hearing my father tell of his uncle who was one of the thousands who perished in Napoleon's army in the retreat from Moscow, and this momentarily suggested I ask him about his father, but I never did.

---

*I was close! Subsequently discovered information reveals that my grandfather was born in 1815—interestingly and to the exact year—100 years before I was born. And my grandmother's birth-year was 1840.

The absence of any reference to his father serves only to underscore the references to his mother, of whom I have most vivid recollections. She was clearly the dominant force in his life and in the life of her family. Nor do I need to guess at this. Among the many recurrences of my father's, "If you want to understand me, you must know. . . .", there was this one, "If you want to understand me, you must have known my mother." This is underscored by the general fact that he thought of himself not so much as a Dykstra as a Vander Schaaf, which was his mother's maiden name. She was a woman of steel, and by my recollection, which may have failed to pick up the finer traits of her personality, she was a woman completely humorless but also completely and positively appealing. My father summarized her character as combining "determination with tireless patience," but surely even more exactly, I think, she was embodied in her own favorite expression, in the Frisian, "Ik seil't wol dwaen," "Then I shall do it myself." Herein lies that peculiar quality of the Frisian freedom instinct, a freedom from letting oneself become dependent, either on circumstances or on other persons. But for me another description came to be etched even more indelibly. She died in August of 1928, of, as I recall, "dropsy," But apparently it had been expected that she might die somewhat before she actually did. I shall never forget an aunt's words as we gathered around her casket: "Grandma died, but not before she decided she was ready"; and that, to me then, was not mere poetry. Knowing her as I had, it was so obviously credible, so credible that I remember how hard I had to work to squeeze out what I supposed were the few properly decorous tears which I could muster at her funeral.

All of this is underscored by my father's reports about the voyage to New York, a voyage then of about twenty days. There were the usual somewhat frightening North Atlantic storms, which they apparently took in stride. But two days out of New York a mammoth explosion wracked the ship, of a proportion which made everyone sure that the ship would sink. "It was in early morning," my father wrote,

and the consternation among the seven hundred passengers was simply indescribable. There was prayer, cursing, and despair. The natural impulse was to rush from the cabins to the decks above. A precious tradition is preserved that Mother Dykstra maintained an unusual calmness of soul and summoned the family around her, exhorting to complete resignation of accepting the awful fate to go down to the deep together.

That story, by the way, was often retold on those occasions on the plains of South Dakota, though much less frightening, when our home was being relentlessly pounded by the terrible wind and hail storms that were common to the plains states. Then father would easily fall into his mother's role at the time of the impending shipwreck. It also accounts for the awed fascination my father had for the story of the later sinking of the Titanic, a book-length account of which served as one of the occasional serial readings at family "devotions." And I rather suspect that this deliverance from the impending disaster (the ship obviously did not go down) came to mean an added confirmation of his own personal consciousness of being "special, with a special mission."

I have mentioned that my father often did use the expression, "if you want to know me, you must. . . ." They are all relevant, but certainly none of them can begin to count for as much as, "If you want to know me, you must have known my mother."

The seven children, besides Mink, who had died in infancy or early boyhood, were named Reintje, Saapke, Reinder, Simon, Broer (my father), Doetje, and Akke. My father's given name was simply the Dutch and Frisian word for "brother." It seems almost ironic that his parents might appear to have run out of ideas for names for him, in view of the fact that his own naming of his progeny is an interesting and imaginative story of its own. His middle name was Doekele, after his father, though his father's name had added an "s", which would have made it the obvious Frisian counterpart of the Scottish Douglas. His college contemporaries used the name "Bert" but it did not stick, and for all except them he simply came to be known as "B. D."

Simon and Doetje I never knew and I have no recollection of their having been talked about, even as far as the circumstances of their relatively early deaths is concerned.

Reintje and Saapke, who became "Aunt Rena" and "Aunt Sarah," I do vividly recall, and every recollection adds up to their image as in every sense of the term "ladies". Aunt Rena was a small, soft-spoken, gentle lady, who lived on as such in her own daughters. She married a farmer, who had come to America on the same ship as my father's family. I knew them only after their retirement from the farm, as they lived in an exquisitely maintained home in a small town not far from the family home at Sioux Center. When later our family made its annual trip from South Dakota to Iowa to visit our Iowa relatives, which included a short stop at Uncle Hessel's home, we hardly dared move a muscle, indoors for fear that some decorative chinaware might come tumbling down from its shelf, or outdoors lest we dislodge a piece of crushed limestone from its border into the lawn which was my Uncle's pride. But let no one be misled by the designation of my Uncle as "farmer"; any later connotation of the farmer as dumb, or boorish, or clumsy, would surely have been shattered by this beautiful couple. Almost exclusively from them did I get to hear, as they rolled in for their frequent visits, the Frisian language in action. And I do mean *action*. Aunt Rena was the lady who reportedly said, ever so gently, as she faced her end, "If there is a God and a heaven, that is all right; and if there isn't, that is all right, too." Her husband had a special interest to us of "pure ears" who listened to the flow of the Frisian because, vigorous in his speech, every sentence seemed to find a natural and appropriate place in it for its own "By golly"—which I for a long time believed was a perfectly proper Frisian expression.

Aunt Sarah was a particularly awesome lady. She had married and gone to live all the way out in San Francisco, which fact gave her all the glamor she needed among us. I have to guess that she "married well," perhaps a businessman. All we got to know about her husband, however, was that he died in the agonies of delirium tremens—which must have had some bearing on my father's subsequent intense opposition to the use of alcoholic beverages in any form. But when Sarah swept in on her occasional visits, it seemed she was all furs and big hats, which was not particularly calculated to put my plainer mother at ease, or my father, either.

The one brother who lived long enough for us to get to know him was Reinder, by any objective standard a rather pathetic individual, made doubly so by comparison with his gracious sisters and my intellectually talented father. To say of him that he was a man of average talents would be an over-generous statement, even if one thought of the talents of an average working man. And he was obviously always most ill at ease in gatherings of the family, though never disdained by them. He sat unobtrusively on the fringes of the crowd, quite unable to converse on even the most commonplace topics. But he, too, found his mission in life, as a part-time church custodian. One part of his responsibility as such was that he ring the church bell daily, at seven, noon, and six o'clock, to mark the time of day for the community. And for year after year, he became famous for never having missed a ringing or been off in his timing. There is a word for that: he rang the bell "religiously." But ringing the bell *was* his religion. For my father, Reinder put meaning into the biblical saying, "Well done, good and faithful servant, you have been faithful in a little thing."

My father's younger sister, who became Agnes, when measured in terms not only of what she was but of what she did, was certainly the crowning jewel of the clan. She shared her sisters' graciousness, their lady-likeness, their soft-spoken charm. But she surely put her own unique stamp on it. For one thing, she was richly cultured, in the educated sense of cultured, much of it self-acquired, all of it ready to bounce out in the form of some timely quotation from one of the classics of our literary heritage. Often when the busy conversation had drifted off, as conversations within family circles will, to border on gossip, there was Aunt Agnes with her gentle crushing put-down, "And now let something kind be said." Visiting her home and discovering that there was one large room, the "library," its walls lined with glass-fronted book cases, whose shelves bore what seemed to me at the time every great literary classic ever produced, helped my impressionable mind toward dreaming of participation in the rich heritage of our literary culture.

Her housekeeping, though the home was well-appointed and spacious, was the despair of my mother who had so much less to work with. Her kitchen eccentricities became legendary. Have you ever known anyone to offer a guest *half* an egg, and strictly not out of penury? And her own appearance, though she could well afford luxury, was a matter of almost total unconcern, a trait she shared with my father. On one famous excursion of some weeks in Europe as she attended an assembly of the World Council of Churches, her baggage always managed to lag a day behind her; it never occurred to her that it might be unusual to manage with only the dress she wore.

Married to a lawyer who was a native of Minnesota, Anthony te Paske, she herself became a lawyer, the first woman to be admitted to the bar in the state of Iowa. So far as I know she acquired her legal preparation not by attending law school but as an apprentice in her husband's office. Together, the two of them were the ones to whom the immigrants first turned for assistance in managing their affairs, and where people could not afford it, there was no charge. Inevitably some cases were lost by them and others to them and their clients and they had occasionally to bear the sting of recrimination. But this was far overshadowed by their mountains of good works. For decades one of my aunt's major projects was to assist newly arrived immigrants in the process of becoming naturalized citizens. The process of preparation went far beyond the mere minimum of helping them to pass the basic naturalization test. It became a thorough effort at enculturation into the America she had come to love with all her heart. And as each new class of immigrants completed the preparation course, she made sure there was an appropriate rite of their passage into the full stream of American life. At her death in an auto accident the year before my father died, the full scope of her activities was for the first time pulled together. She was a major force in the work of the Womens' Christian Temperance Union. In her church she was much less anxious about maintaining some ecclesiastical purity than in seeking the well-being of persons. No community improvement project had occurred in which she was not involved—anything that was "pure, lovely, and of good reputation" attracted her enthusiastic support. She was a major reinforcement for my father in innumerable ways, and when she died something very, very big went out of his life. She was truly one of the great ladies I have known.

These, plus those we never knew, were the family that came over from Friesland. With an original intent to settle near Orange City, Iowa, they were hindered in that by a smallpox quarantine that was in effect and were diverted to Sioux Center, twelve miles to the northwest. And from that time and for the rest of his life, Sioux Center became for my father the emotional center of his universe. Though he never lived there after his teens, he returned many years later to be married in the Old First Church of Sioux Center. When a son died in infancy while we lived in South Dakota, he was buried in the cemetery across the street from the church. And when my father died, and later my mother, they too returned to his "true home" to be buried there.

The transplanting from Friesland was thus emotionally complete. Only at one time and fairly late in his life, and only when for a brief instant there seemed to be a chance to return, did there ever seem to be any wish to go back to where he had come from, or, for that matter, any trace of nostalgia for Friesland. In another of the analogies to which he was so alert, he saw himself another veritable Abraham, going out in faith and in faith arriving at his promised land; or, in another favorite phrase, he took seriously the admonition, "Let him who puts his hand to the plow not look back."

Speaking of the plow does provide a nice transition from the story of the emigration to the farm which the family was able to purchase, just a few miles west of Sioux Center. The thought of owning an Iowa farm did not then conjure up today's visions of an enormous investment, but relative to the times, the fact that they were able to purchase a farm, and a fairly sizable one (eventually four hundred and forty acres) for those pre-mechanized times is an indication that financially the family came out of the Netherlands depression in fairly good shape. At any rate, the little boy who had wandered carefree along the Frisian dikes was now translated into "a farm boy from Iowa."

I am in no way committed to a kind of circumstantial determism which would hold that in what we become we are merely the pawns in the hands of the conditions that befall us, or the effects of causes. What we become we become at least in significant measure by our freedom, to suppress some things and encourage others. But once a life is complete, a *fait accompli*, and we try to understand its meanings we have to turn to a reading of the changing circumstances to arrive at an accurate estimate of things. So in this case. There is no way of understanding some of the large things that appear down the road without seeing that farm-boy experience and understanding exactly what it was and was not.

There is an almost total lack of detail. In a brief chronology which my father wrote, there appears the item: "1882-1889—on the farm. Common school." What that at least does say is that he did not move directly from elementary school to secondary. Indeed, he was approaching his eighteenth birthday when he began secondary school. There had to be some four years, therefore, during which he was not in school but at work full-time on the farm. This makes the paucity of his reference to life on the farm even a little more surprising.

What the few details there are about those seven years do make clear is that life had now become fairly difficult, whatever it may have been in Friesland. One is tempted to look back to those days through the lenses of our own, when possession of a 440-acre farm in Iowa is for ordinary folk a nearly mind-boggling guarantee of wealth. Then it surely was not so. Nor did this fall into the modern cliche of farmers living poor but dying rich since their wealth is in their land which they can sell only at the end. Somewhere in the late eighties or early nineties, and most probably at my grandfather's death, the land was disposed of, but my grandmother was apparently left in part dependent for financial support on my father, who himself made only trifling wages. It is safe to say, I think, that from that time on and for all his life my father not only thought of himself as poor but actually was in fact up against what he generally called, in Darwin's phrase in another context, "Het strijd om het bestaan," "the struggle for survival." If we sometimes over the years wondered whether father's poverty seemed to be in a way wilful, a contrived poverty which might enable him to indulge in the secret pride of having to be so humble about things, then that was surely not wholly so.

A little more surprisingly, as far as those seven years are concerned, we discover that his earlier sense of being specially endowed intellectually was at least dormant, if not gone. One would expect to find some evidence of the continuance of the flaming vision which nourished itself through daily hardships by one's vowing that some day it would be gained. And if his mother had indeed heard what the schoolmaster had said on the wharves of Harlingen, there is no sign that she had turned it into a deep commitment to her supposedly singled-out son. No serious thought seemed to have been given to getting on with further schooling of a formal sort, though every spare moment, even in the interstices between the routine operations during the day, was given to poring over books. If anything is clear, it is that farming seemed to be simply appealing (after a quick thought about becoming a bank clerk) and not simply something he might be doing because preferred options were closed at least temporarily.

He spoke of the actual work on the farm, but not as if in complaint. There is a mention of a forty acre field of grain, and apparently the responsibility at harvest fell wholly on him and his brothers. This almost certainly had to involve the process of "shocking" the grain, gathering the tied bundles which the reaper had dropped randomly and standing them upright leaning against each other in collections of eight or ten, partly to allow a run-off of water should rain fall and partly to allow the ripened heads of grain to dry more completely in preparation for the threshing. This assumes that at that time there were machines in use which did the cutting of the grain and the tying into bundles, and threshing machines.

"Shocking" was indeed hard work. But there was another side to it as well. It was one of the things that could be done by boys even in their lower and pre-teens—one of the things which, different from such lighter chores as gathering the eggs or tending the calves, gave one a feeling that he was now doing pretty nearly a man's work. That this went on for the full day added to the feeling of manliness about it. Shocking, therefore, carried with it some of the thrill of being a rite of passage—from boyhood to manhood, like graduating from sitting on one side of the center aisle in church with mother to moving to the other side to sit with the men-folk. So no one ever thought to complain about or even mention the intolerable aching of the muscles not yet quite up to the task or the bone-weariness which kept one awake at night.

And if the farm boy was involved in shocking grain at harvest time, it is a pretty safe assumption that he was otherwise also engaged in reasonably strenuous tasks. But if it is exactly that that forms an image of being a farm-boy in Iowa, then my father, as we knew him later, was never really a farm boy at heart. He did constantly extol, later, the virtues of physical toil and had all kinds of nice things to say about those whose lives were spent at it. But in so far as it involved such toil, farming simply was not quite in his nature. For one thing he hardly had the physical stature to keep up with the pace. People at five foot four and a hundred and twenty pounds were hardly the farmer type. For all his physical activity he was not particularly physically adept—everything he did was rather makeshift. Later—and until he was past eighty he lived at least on a small farm—and fortunately he did not have to do the work since he had had the foresight to produce a crop of sons to do it for him. But how he loved to supervise, to leave orders for the work to be done that day! During his years as editor he was accustomed to leaving the house for the office at seven in the morning, and we got to developing an interesting little game (to which even mother became a party) of placing nominal bets on how often he would leave only to return to announce an additional little order or two.

But if my father was short on the capacity and instinct to be the working farmer which he loved to extol for others, he made up for it by being very long on something else. He loved the land! And even that is understatement. All his life, after his education was completed, he managed to own his own land, and for much more than the economic reason that it was a good investment and a means for providing for the family's basic material needs. Owning land met for him a very basic psychological need. He loved the old Greek myth of the monster who drew his strength from contact with the soil, so that the key to overcoming him was to raise him off the ground and hold him there. He saw some connection between the old saying, "Give me a lever and a fulcrum and I'll move the world," and his own relation to the ground. One of the things that drew him into spiritual kinship with the Russian peasant was Tolstoi's portrayal of the ineffable link he had to the soil. Owning land had sacramental value. So did everything that grew, be it flower or weed or tree or insect or fowl or beast. He knew, and not merely by reading Schweitzer, all about "the reverence for life." Later he was to become the veritable Johnny Appleseed of his area of the South Dakota flatlands, as he made a passion of planting trees wherever there was a bare spot. In that sense he was in the deepest way a farmer at heart.

I have no doubt that this aspect of his life provided him with an always needed and always welcomed balance to and rejuvenation of the otherwise hyperactive life of his mind. When he worked it had to be at something light and wholly routine. When the wells of his mind ran dry, he got out not a book but his faithful hoe and in the act of hoeing would start the juices flowing again. In this lay his version of being at the same time *of* nature and *over* nature, the place where nature and spirit meet.

There is no extant information as to exactly what were the circumstances of the disposition of the farm or when it was sold. The next dated segment in the chronology which he left behind speaks of his education, beginning with his entry into secondary school in 1889, at the age of nearly eighteen. And by at least that slight indication schooling was henceforth to command his attention. But remembering his comment, "I am wherever I have been," that surely has to include the years on the farm. Or as we used to say, "Once you have been a farm boy in Iowa you'll never be the same again."

III
"Education"

And now he was back in pursuit of what then and afterwards he was to see as his life's preferred task—education. There is no more reference to life on the Sioux Center farm. What happened to it or to his family remains a blank page. That may be simply due to an unplanned negligence on his part as he wrote his sketches of reminiscence. For that matter, just what does one write about life on the farm? Its routines were demanding but mainly routines even so. The years followed other years, each defined by its crucial episodes of seed-time and harvest, all of it touched by anxiety or relief at the treatment which the physical environment afforded. But there were people involved, at least the family. And one could wish for much more detail as to the eventual dispersion of the family as each member rose to maturity and left to live his or her own life. If the farm was disposed of as a result of grandfather's old age and the death of Simon, the brother, which combined to deplete the supply of manpower to carry out its many functions, it would be good to know what after that the family's circumstances or life-style might have been. The only thing there is information on is the formal education process, which, in the chronological list, occupied the years from 1889 until 1902—from the beginning of secondary school through a year at Yale.

Even the venture into secondary school was not the routine, virtually automatic and mostly universal step we know it as today. Few children went on beyond the eighth grade. Children were, after all, from the time they were thirteen or fourteen, a valuable and needed asset in carrying on the work of the farm. And in a stable community of disciplined, serious people like Sioux Center, the education acquired during the eight or nine years of elementary school was sure to be of a reasonably adequate quality to insure an ability not only to do the work of the farm very ably but to participate meaningfully in the social and cultural life of the community, centered there chiefly in the life of the churches.

My father entered his secondary education phase by attending the then existing Northwestern Classical Academy. This school was the forerunner of what is now Northwestern College in Orange City. It was a school operated by the Reformed Church in America, and one of several such academies which that church (and other denominations) had established as they moved westward. There were academies in Holland, Michigan, in German Valley, Illinois, in Cedar Grove, Wisconsin, and later my father was to establish one in South Dakota, under the auspices and with the support of the area churches. It is not wholly clear what was the status of such academies, particularly in the Reformed Church. In the case of a parallel Dutch denomination, the Christian Reformed Church, the academies were emphatically parochial, being built on a substructure of parochial elementary schools. The idea of parochial elementary schools on the part of the Reformed Churches not only never took hold but was, rather surprisingly, objected to by many and with considerable vigor, apparently not for any mundanely economic considerations. In the Reformed Churches the academies had a hard time convincing the church constituencies of their importance, and in later years when larger percentages of people extended their educations beyond the eighth grade many more students from the Reformed Churches attended the existing public high schools than the academies. Most fundamentally this difference between the stricter parochialism of the Christian Reformed churches as compared to the Reformed Church reflects different temperamental dispositions toward the whole emigration idea and toward what later came to be identified as "secular" culture. In the one case, emigration amounted to an aim simply to move the culture, which had been threatened by the state church in the Netherlands, to another locale where it could preserve itself intact against any such threat. In the other case, emigration was a step en route to becoming part of another culture, the then unfolding free culture of America.

That complexity in the notion of the "academy" is but a part of the complexity involved in trying to determine what the fact that my father attended the academy in Orange City said about him, or his mother, at that time. His later experience in education, public and parochial, and his reflections on it form a very complex mosaic, and I am not sure he ever did reduce the issue to neat terms even though the many things he did say he said in his usual vociferous way.

But all of this happened within the contexts of at least one thing that was clear: education, in whatever form or under whatever auspices, stood at the top or at least very near to the top of life's priorities, not merely as a vocation for himself but as a priority for people generally. And if there was a second clarity it was only scarcely less prior than the first: it was that religion had a large stake in the fostering of education, though it is far less clear whether in this case the aim of education is finally the reinforcement or protection of the religious parochialism or simply one expression of religion's impulse to foster a general enlargement of life—the art of living well.

The decision to attend the Academy in Orange City certainly was not without its attendant practical hardships, which suggests that it had to be a decision not lightly made. If the family then lived still on the farm at Sioux Center, this would entail a daily round trip of some thirty miles. The Academy was no boarding school and I have no information about any regular provision available at the time for assisting students in getting to and from school. There conceivably were arrangements by which persons attending the Academy could live in nearby private homes. And if I stretch my memory as far back as it will go, I do seem to remember as a vague possibility that my father may have resided with a family named Bolks. But that is certainly too nebulous to be made much of, and derives whatever credibility it might have from the circumstance that I cannot imagine how else he might have managed. Later on, under similar circumstances, in South Dakota, he relied on horseback riding. But had he done that in prep school days, I am sure we would have been regaled somewhere along the line with tales of those heroic days when, even through the rugged days of a northwest Iowa winter, he manfully rode his horse two hours to and two hours from school.

What gives point to this much speculation about an otherwise trivial matter is that, if one could know clearly what prompted his attending the Academy, that might offer a clue which could unravel the complexity of some of his later thinking about education. Later (and I am sure it was only later) he became quite adamant about the special merits of what to us is the parochial school. What is complex is what his special reasons for advocacy of it were. And depending on how that is answered what is to us "parochial" might turn out to be for him not parochial at all.

A couple of speculations about what might have been a key influence in determining that he should go to the Academy can be mentioned, but mainly to put them on the agenda so that they can be of some use in understanding some other things down the line. One is that the Academy was a preparatory school for those intending to go into one of the church's vocations. This image of the Academy is abetted both by the fact that it happened and by the fact that it became a major promotion item for the school—that many of its graduates did enter the church vocations, as ministers and missionaries. But apparently in my father's case, his interest in a church vocation did not arise until after he was in college, and even then, as his selection of academic interests reveals, it does not seem to have been very clearcut. His mother, I remember his saying, had at one time mentioned, though clearly in a casual way which was not at the time at all persuasive, that she would like to see him become a minister. But it is hard to find anything to support the notion that he entered the Academy with that as his intention.

Some people, I am sure, and at least later, were in effect fooled by the name "Classical Academy." What that seemed to indicate was a stress on a certain kind of education. It pointed to an association, in the minds of the somewhat more sophisticated, with the "classical" civilizations of Greece and Rome, along with a stress on learning Greek and Latin. And beyond that, this sounded something like being safely traditional. Even as early as then, before public education had taken on its more typically pragmatic emphasis, "classical" carried an appeal reminiscent of the appeal the New England prep schools were to have in contrast to the public high schools. That reading of the term "classical" may have thus had some fortuitous consequences for a place like the Academy. But the term had nothing to do with the type of educational emphasis that was given. It derived from the fact that the sponsoring bodies were "Classes," an official ecclesiastical area consortium of churches, or, in the case of Northwestern Academy, of a group of three classes.

Of my father's academic career at the Academy, the only thing there is to report is that he simply performed at the highest levels in everything. We have not only his word for it or hearsay: the transcripts of credits and grades are among his papers. One cannot, by looking over the list of courses, learn anything about where his academic interests lay, since there simply was no room in a curriculum that had to serve so small a school for any elections such as might have provided hints as to his special interests. There was a great deal of Greek and Latin, but Greek and Latin were simply what anyone studied who went to an Academy—or, for that matter and at that time, to a high school. There is no particular mention of any teacher who might have made a special impression. By at least the usual mind-set of the day, one did not naturally discriminate among one's teachers which might have been a "good" teacher or a "poor" one (though one did remember who was "strict" and who was not). Teachers, by virtue of having been identified as teachers, seem to have been endowed with an aura which discouraged critical judgment. And my father did live in awe of them. I do not know what the teaching profession in general may have looked like in those days, but the teachers even in so remote a place as the Academy in Iowa were impressive persons. By comparison with them I think we may find today's sterotype of the high school teacher quite distinctly shallow. Teachers who at one time or another taught at the Academy became honored names in the larger life of the Reformed Church, not merely as a *pro forma* gesture but because of their substantive merit. And the significant professional achievements of their students, then largely in church vocations as parish ministers and missionaries, were a live testimonial to their stature.

There is just one clue as to what my father's main academic interest may have been (and by stretching that dangerously far, one can risk seeing it as a possible clue as to what at that time he might have envisioned for himself). It is hard to date what period in his academic career that might have referred to but as good a guess as any is that it did refer to Academy days. It is a reference to his exceptional interest and aptitude in mathematics. No assignment was ever left unfinished, no problem ever went unsolved. Not only that, but there was, however fleeting, a toying with the dream of eventually attending Amherst to obtain his doctorate in mathematics! That it was to be Amherst shows that he was at least sophisticated enough in his awareness of the larger academic world to know that there was an Amherst. Yale or Harvard or Princeton, yes, but Amherst? I am not at all sure that during my sheltered days at the Academy fifty years later I would have known there was an Amherst. And that it was to be mathematics is surprising in the light of and of the directions that his later academic interests took. In another way, I suppose, it may not have been surprising. It surely is not uncommon for the specially gifted mind to suppose that because it is specially gifted it must and can attain to the finishedness, the compact neatness, of a mathematical demonstration. But what is of interest in the dream of a mathematical doctorate from Amherst is that it is the only reference there is to a special academic and eventual vocational interest during his Academy years; and this only reference we have does not point to his eventual interests in languages, or theology, or to a church vocation.

It would be a deplorable neglect to end this quick account of the Academy days without also adding that the Academy, and subsequently the Junior College and the College which that initial venture grew into, remained until his death an object of special affection. The Academy's alumni generally have always been powerfully attached to that first of their alma maters. But no one, I think, loved the institution more deeply than my father did, above any other alma mater he was yet to come to know.

From there it was on to Hope College in Michigan. There certainly could be no puzzlements about that move. Moving from the Reformed

Church's Academy to its Hope College was as natural as moving up from a minor league club to its parent club. There is no evidence (and I think I would find it hard to believe it if I saw it) that any other alternative was considered. Nor is there evidence that my father seriously considered not going on to college at all, though circumstances were to become such that he almost did not make it. At any rate the move from the Academy to Hope College was clearly the path of least resistance. It was by "the path of least resistance" that all of his major circumstantial determinations were made, however vigorous and agressive and against-the-tide he may have been in how he handled the circumstances once he was settled into them.

It is clear that in his college days the academic juices were flowing as strongly as they ever had in old Friesland. The Academy years had whetted his appetite for more. He seems to have settled into the academic routines with full gusto. The paucity of his references, either in his conversations or his extant papers, to such matters as the details of his living conditions, of his travelling back and forth from home to campus, of what may have been his social life—this has conspired to leave something of an image of him during those years as if he were a kind of disembodied brain simply there to absorb the intellectualia, a "loner" absorbed only in his private intellectual pursuits. But there is in such few references as he has left enough evidence to suggest that he was a lively participant in at least some part of the life of the campus. And as I recall his later interactions with his former schoolmates as they visited in our home or in their letters to him, they pointed to his having been in a healthy sense very much one of them. But that circle of intimates was always a small one.

If there were any special inhibitions that kept him apart, they were again largely those imposed by economic hardship, which was to be the abiding story of his life. Somewhere in those years he had, mainly by way of accelerating his education, found time to do some elementary school teaching, for which he had received the princely sum of thirty-seven dollars a month. And some of that had gone to help support his then widowed mother. But with that and what little he was able to earn by farm work during his summer vacations he had to make his way through college. He did live at least for part of that time in a room in the college dormitory, Van Vleck Hall. There each room was equipped with its own little pot-bellied stove but the students were responsible for providing their own wood to keep the stoves going. I have no imformation as to how this was generally managed but for my father it meant spending a good part of his weekends scrounging for firewood, going out as far as a place called Pine Creek, which is still there, a good four miles our from the campus. Even so, and to conserve his energies and fuel, he generally simply wrapped himself in blankets as he worked at his studies. How throughout his life he managed his fuel problems would make quite a saga by itself—interesting now in the face of our fuel shortages and our anxieties about them.

The positive thing about his college years is that here he again clearly excelled as a student by virtue of a natural intellectual talent but not without the exercise of a constant and sacrificial discipline. And this was not simply by hearsay. His college transcript bears this out. The whole process was enlivened by the fact that throughout the four years he was locked in a fierce (and I hope friendly) competition academically with a generally acknowledge eccentric genius, Edward Dimnent, who was later to become the college's president, and incidentally to make a fortune in the stock market *during* the years of the Great Depression (rumor has it that the Chicago stock brokers were calling *him* for tips during those years). A comparison of the two transcripts bears this out. No one was ever ahead of the other by more than a nose, but each day it was a toss-up as to whose nose it would be. This was not merely a private war but it was generally recognized and reportedly provided an interesting sideshow for the students in the various classes. Whether it was always a friendly rivalry I have no way of knowing, but I do know that in later years some mutual venom did creep into the relationship— maybe the only instance there was of that kind of thing entering a relation between my father and someone else.

The course of study was again a broad one, with not enough room for academic selections to indicate what special directions my father's interests might be taking. The evidence there is points to his having been pretty much equally spontaneously interested in everything that came along: literature, classical languages, history, mathematics, the natural sciences. In later years he spoke much less of the courses of study he had taken and more of the teachers he had taken them from, and he clearly became aware that in teaching the teacher is more significant than the subject matter. He spoke of having "gotten," not chemistry but Yntema, not biology but Patterson, not Greek but Gillespie, not mathematics but Kleinheksel. In this there seems to have been revived in him the favourable image of the stature of the teacher, such as he had once felt in the schoolmaster in Friesland. And he declares that he went through all of this "with no definite calling in mind." For him the academic life was clearly not a pre-something else. It was a life intrinsically satisfying.

But while he was thus revelling in the life of a scholar, something else was also happening on the side and by way partly of extra-curricular influences. He was taking note of the specifically Christian character of the men who were his teachers, and in his extra-curricular involvements he found himself gravitating toward an involvement in the student Christian associations. Organized athletics for all of his life was one of the main targets of his attack. Athletics was not merely not for him, it was not for anyone else either. The last letter I received from him, written but a few days before he died, was a tirade against a certain minister whom we both knew well, for the fact that he had let his son become a basketball player (and what was worse, a very good one). Each of us sons has his own story to tell of sneaking out of the house at night "to go to study in the library," only to end up playing some tiny role in some athletic contest. Nor was college-style partying looked on with any greater favour, and in this he went far beyond the not uncommon skepticism with which parents look upon the party tendencies of their offspring. There were college "fraternities" on the campus at the time, but fortunately, in his eyes, these were then wholly designed as literary societies" (which over the years did cover a multitude of hardly literary items) where students read prepared papers for the edification (?) of their peers. But the organized "Christian" associations were the thing, and indeed were given an official priority rating both by the members of the faculty and the students.

It was by a combination of the influences, much more by example than by overt utterances or any direct attempts to proselytize for a profession, of his teachers and the involvement in the Christian association that my father's interests gradually came to focus on the possibility of an eventual church vocation. He singles out for special attention one occasion when he had given a speech at the weekly meeting of the Christian student group. After that one of his teachers, Gillespie from the Greek department, had kind words to say about the speech, and specifically urged him on the strength of his speaking ability to consider entering the Christian ministry. And J. B. Nykerk, who at the very end of his career forty years later was to be my teacher, too, offered some special plaudits for the excellence of the speech. Plaudits from Nykerk were special because they were so rare; he had acquired so great a fame as something of an eccentric tyrant taskmaster, spanning the teaching both of music and the forensic arts, that a favorable word from him had all the force of being a sign from heaven. The applause for my father had special meaning to him because it appears it was the first time ever that he had realized that he *could* speak and speak well. In the course of praising him for his speech Nykerk also seems to have mentioned the possibility of my father's considering the ministry as his life vocation.

Others, perhaps more casually, had spoken of it but Nykerk's mention seems to have been the decisive one.

There is certainly no sense in which this could be called a religious conversion. It simply represented a coming to clarity, and fairly casually, as to what vocation he might pursue. That also did not happen as if he had been in any kind of inner turmoil over the question. He simply had not given the matter much thought. And then there it was, the easy coming together of a number of gentle and unplanned influences, all now conjoined to the evidence that that might be where his talents lay, the talent most specifically of speaking. And that did fit the image of the minister in those days: far different from today's image of the minister as a dozen-sided genius, it mattered mainly (or only) that a minister could speak well.

There was an early rumor among members of the family which, because my father nowhere makes mention of it, had to be at least half apocryphal, that somewhere in his reflections as to where in the church vocations he might find his special niche he did entertain the notion of going as a missionary to China. (Among us, that lived on only as the light-hearted banter, "Heavens! we might have been Chinese!") By the rumor, the reason that that fell through was my mother's health-condition. That would have dated the possibility of being a missionary to China much later, and late enough to have been the effect on my father of the great missionary movement of the first decade of this century, with its "evangelizing the world in this generation" slogan. What is probably decisive in reducing that part of the story wholly to mythology is that so far as any of us could know, my mother always enjoyed (until her late years) an excellent and robust health.

But with college in that way having provided the focus for his life's work, there certainly was no problem about what should come after college. Western Seminary was, after all, just across the street, but he did not cross that street routinely or at once. He completed his college work somewhat before the end of the normal four years and then went home to Iowa and taught for a few months in the local country elementary school. When he went to turn in the key to the school at the end of the term he walked away instead with a contract to teach for the next year as well. This was prompted only in part by economic necessity. As importantly he returned because of his sheer joy in teaching. From a later perspective it was hard to see any congruity between his own intellectual interests and talent on the one hand and the image of him as teacher of an elementary school, even keeping in mind his own image of the schoolmaster in Frisia to look up to. For at least north European immigrants the schoolmaster was held in an esteem second only to that of the minister, an esteem not quite matched in the traditional male chauvinist mind for the American "school-marm." But the thought of such possible incongruity did not only not bother him, it seems never to have occurred to him. At the same time being back home gave him an opportunity to be with his mother who had then left the farm, and to share his own meager income for her support.

But finally it was off to Seminary where he plunged once more into the world of academe, with possibly even more austerity than before as far as maintaining himself physically was concerned. He "managed his own boarding" but in the memoir does not add that his one staple of food was oatmeal. So much was that a part of him that the Quaker Oats Company should have struck a medal in his memory. This severe hardship was, however, in part self-imposed, since he simply refused to take advantage of available, and apparently quite readily available, scholarship funds. He records his dismay at how extravagant his fellow students were in their use of these. But his attitude toward "things" really deserves a separate chapter.

It is also clear that he entered upon Seminary work without any delusions of grandeur about himself, and without even a great deal of confidence in himself, despite the fact that he was now nearing his twenty-eighth birthday. It was customary for the Seminary to send its students out during the summer vacations and on week-ends during the school term to serve as student ministers in the various parishes. He considered that it would have been much too presumptive for him to have accepted such assignments.

Seminary in one sense did not arouse in him the same kind of enthusiasm that college had. College years were highlighted by the great people who were his teachers, and he had unbridled admiration for them. Although he was ready to acknowledge the competence of his Seminary teachers, he also was not a little bit scandalized by the atmosphere of jealousy that prevailed among them. And he never was able to forget or forgive one of them (let us call him "John") who on one occasion when he failed to get his way simply sat down and wept. To belittle *anyone* was simply not in my father's make-up, but for at least this once there was an incomparable sneer in his voice as he later recalled, "And Johnnie" (who became one of the more celebrated giants in the church's esteem) "Johnnie sat down and cried." This was not the sole or major cause, but it was at least one consideration, I think, which must explain my father's lifelong disposition to hold seminaries at least at arm's length. He never showed the admiration for his teachers there that he had for those at Northwestern Academy or his college or for the Seminary as an institution.

Again the Seminary curriculum was quite short on elective options, so one cannot read from his course selections where his own specific interests within the theological spectrum lay. I have to locate the source of his later extraordinary fascination with languages in his seminary study of Hebrew and Greek, partly because there is no indication earlier that his interest in languages was anything more than routine, and partly because when he did later go on to Yale, he did opt to study mainly languages.

The one thing that does emerge as special during his seminary years was his recognition as a preacher, and a recognition that was borne out by his lifelong reputation specifically as a pulpiteer, though cast in a different mold than most recognized pulpiteers. There were, interestingly, two quite different schools of judgment about his preaching. Upon hearing one of his student sermons one of his teacher critics is reported to have exclaimed: "For the *Bibliotheca-Sacra*, excellent! for the pulpit, never!" (The *Bibliotheca-Sacra* was at that time the most prominent scholarly journal for theological studies and famous among students for how dull it was.) But another of his teacher-critics equally vigorously exclaimed: "Stupendous! that sermon would fit equally in the pulpit of Marble Collegiate Church (on Fifth Avenue in New York) and in the pulpit of the most remote outpost-parish of the prairies!" (In the pre-Norman Vincent Peale days, Marble Church was more famous for its scholarly preaching than for its "positive thinking"). On one score the first judgment is doubtful. I cannot imagine my father ever writing anything to match the typical *Bibliotheca-Sacra* in the typical research-based style of its articles. I shall reserve elaborating on the second until later, when it will be appropriate to say something about my father's speaking styles.

At the end of the seminary years, my father was designated the class speaker at commencement time, an honor that usually went to the outstanding scholars of the class. There were two such speakers, one to deliver an oration in English, my father in Dutch. He delivered his oration on the topic "Theology as Queen of the Sciences." What prompted him to speak on that topic is hard to detect, but at the least it had to express his own sense of priority now for the study of theology, seeing all his previous and wide-ranging intellectual interests now committed toward serving her.

By an interesting coincidence (and contrast) when I stood exactly in the same position thirty-eight years later, my own oration bore the title, "The Divine Contradiction." Where his happened in the context of the larger image of all knowledge forming a system reaching its apex in the idea of God, mine saw the meaning of God exactly in the contradiction (and transcending) of all systems. Where his saw the meaning of everything as pointing beyond itself to the divine, mine was to find the meaning of everything in simply being what it is. If his, quite unconsciously (for there is no evidence that in his studies he had had any opportunity to become familiar with what was then the hottest item in philosophy) reflected the current tides of Absolute Idealism insofar as that dreamed of all knowledge forming a system with God at its apex, mine equally unconsciously (I was not to discover Soren Kierkegaard until a couple of years later) reflected the coming Existentialist antagonism to systems and the extolling of the individual and the particular.

So Seminary ended, and again, a deviation from the normal pattern of moving directly from completion of professional training into the settled church vocation. This delay seems to have been by choice. He did want to fulfill a long cherished dream of attending a graduate school. So he accepted an appointment to serve for the summer as the minister of a small parish in New Sharon, Iowa. But summers had for him an uncanny way of stretching out into a year. The time spent in New Sharon, as it quite unexpectedly developed, would turn out to be one of his most fateful sojourns. We will hear more about New Sharon later.

His reasons for going on to some graduate study beyond completion of the normal professional ministerial preparation are not exactly clear, not because we do not know but because it is not clear which of two things he said about it weighed most heavily. One of his accounts insists that he did not yet feel adequately equipped to assume the responsibilities of a parish ministry, and that he went on to the university in order better to qualify himself. For one so inclined, he certainly chose an odd assortment of courses during his year at Yale (unless he had specific designs on sometime occupying a professorate in a seminary). His concentration was on languages—Arabic and Hebrew and Semitic languages generally, which is understandable enough. But something new was in the picture: Sanskrit. What that suggests is that the interest in languages, not as a means to something else but as an end in itself, had become more lively. Sanskrit, the classical language of India, was not just a language among languages. Where languages generally develop simply by usage, Sanskrit was purportedly something of an artificial language, a language deliberately and systematically invented, and thus an excellent topic for study for anyone wanting to fine-tune his theory about the nature of language. The Sanskrit quite clearly was not studied because it was the door that would lead into the vast and vastly

Education

different world of Hindu culture. Though he had, as I shall note, an extraordinary esteem for Mahatma Gandhi, that did not imply an interest in Hindu traditions of literature and thought-modes (had he come to know the Bhagavad-Gita I am sure he would have been spell-bound by it). There are scant references to Hindu thought later on in his writings, but these seem there only to be rejected. Besides the excursions into language, his year at Yale included his only formal contact with philosophy, as he studied systematic metaphysics under the great Professor George T. Ladd.

I find much more plausible still another reason for his attending Yale than either the enhancement of his professional ministerial competences or the study of languages. His other stated reason was simply "the dream of breathing the air of a great university." (He says that he chose Yale because he had seen a picture of it in his school geography book! He certainly was not the first or last to have his career shaped by the pictures in elementary geography books.) This I can believe much more easily, particularly as I sensed his sheer ecstasy as he returned to Yale's campus for the first time forty-five years later to share my own commencement—that was like a return to Eden. Had he stood before Sinai when Moses spoke, he could not have listened more raptly than as he listened to the President's commencement address. He was a long time coming down to earth after that.

IV
The Golden Age

In the fall, after completion of his one year of study at Yale, he found his first vocational opportunity in a quite unexpected place. This was out in the as yet quite undeveloped area of Platte and Harrison, South Dakota. This was slightly east of the Missouri and not far from the Nebraska border. Dakota was to be his home for the next quarter of a century, and possibly more than any place he had or would live, primarily his "homeland." And more of what he was has to be read in that context than in any other.

But why Dakota? That question has to be, for the moment at least, read not merely as a quest for an explanation of how it happened that he got there. Far more revealingly, the question had a very different connotation, one not without its own deep poignacy. For that other meaning, it read rather, "What is a man like that doing in a place like that?"

It is not clear whether in those early years he was asking that question of himself. I am inclined to think not, though all I have to go by is that, by his own description of the enormous schedule of work he carried on, he could not have found the time for it. And even in retrospect he seems to have been at that time able to work with so warm a feeling of fulfillment that he may not have had any inclination to ask it. Later, yes, as I shall point out, and then I think in a somewhat out-of-character time, but not at the time.

But the public, more or less overtly, seemed to be asking it, and he was sometimes proudly and sometimes painfully aware that they were—which, in a way, may have been more painful than had he been asking it himself of himself. For whatever reason, his being there seemed incongruous. It may have centered simply in the fact that he had, after all, studied at Yale, and the people, though far from the center of things, were not so benighted that they had no sense of what having been at Yale was supposed to say about a person. But they were also sure, as most middle class people are, that *theirs* was "the real world" as compared to the ivory towers of Academe, so they were not disposed to go into a swoon before even a Yale man. Nor did the sense of incongruity

The Golden Age

arise out of a sense of the failure of my father to communicate with them. Such communication with the common people seems to have been his strongest point, and a beautiful recent letter from an eighty-nine year old lady in Yankton, South Dakota, may well have been speaking for a consensus when she recalls hearing my father speak and remarks even now about the clarity of the ideas to which he gave expression. I have clear recollections from my earliest years of the apparent comfort with which he mingled with people, despite at least some indications that he felt socially shy. If anything the sense of incongruity in his being where he was may have been simply an honest expression of their respect for what they saw in him. But it may not always have come through like that. There are some remembered intimations that the public sense of his being someone special might slip the very little distance it would have to slip to become a public sense of his being simply eccentric.

Nor was the sense of incongruity merely confined to his own community, and it was not something he had conjured up out of his own imagination. It had reached further out than that—to Michigan, for one example. And in that context there did occur one particular experience that was to prove to be about as devastating as any in his life. He was a most resilient person and mainly by dint of sheer self-disciplining of his wants he could rise above his adversities. But this once his best resources appeared to have failed to give him his usual lift.

Somewhere, I think it must have been in the twenties, because I was old enough to know of it at the time, he did make application for a teaching position at his college alma mater. This kind of thing came very hard for him—to ask anything of anyone. It may have been because of his natural shyness, but more probably it was something else. He could never quite divorce the notion of taking an initiative to ask something of someone from the notion of being a beggar, and among whatever else my father was he surely was in his way too fiercely proud to be caught in any act of begging. What made it especially difficult to bring himself to the point of asking on this occasion was that the request had now to go to his old college rival, Edward Dimnent. He obviously had special difficulty in seeing himself go hat-in-hand to that somewhat haughty man. But somehow he did manage to bring himself to that point.

That his application was refused, as it turned out, was not itself the point so much as the manner of the refusal. I have two versions of what were given as the reasons for the refusal, one from my recollection from the time and one from his own later account. My own recollection is exact, even to the words my father used in telling me of it. Dimnent had written, he said, that "there is no way in which I could get the nomination of a pacifist to a faculty position past the Board of Trustees"—which, whether true or not, had all the earmarks of a cowardly exit by hiding behind the Trustees. My father's own account in a late memoir has a quite different version. By that account Dimnent had written that the reason he could not now give him a position on his faculty was that he had "gone off and thrown his life away in South Dakota." If that version is correct, then it embodies the cruelest of ironies which it is surprising that Dimnent did not recognize, for it was an act of condemning my father *to* exactly what he condemned him *for*. But that was not all. As if to give the already cruel blade one more cruel twist, Dimnent also went on to express his strong hope that my father would never see fit to send any of his sons to Hope College. (Six of us hold degrees from there.) My father surely could not be blamed for reading this as an act of sheer malice on the part of his old rival. A more charitable and probably more correct version of it, at least for us who were to get to know Dimnent later, would attribute this response to his personal gruffness, an image which was not only there but which he seemed to have delighted in fostering. This entailed on his part a natural insensitivity to the feelings of other persons, in this case the person on the receiving end of his letter which denied the application for a teaching position. But this my father never forgot or forgave; he was greatly embittered by it. I know of no other instance where he ever said anything derogatory about anyone. But in this case he left a vicious comment about Dimnent that will not bear repeating.

Had it not been for this single real-life encounter, my father's image of himself as really destined to be in some important lectureship at a great university but doomed to the prairies of South Dakota might, I think, have been translatable into the relative harmlessness of a recurring and not always painless fantasy. It was this one occasion of being hit hard by it that kept the image alive to bother him. It is clear that he thought about it frequently.

It is hard to know just how much it may have bothered him. The Dimnent episode is spoken of in the context of an unpublished novel he wrote in 1948, a novel which was less novel than autobiography, when he was nearing eighty. In my mother's handwriting on the title page appears the imprimatur, "This is the true story of our lives." But it is remotely possible that though the novel was described as a factually correct account it twisted a few things a bit for dramatic effect. Tragedy does make better reading than light-heartedness, though this is not quite so clearly the case if the tragedy is real-life and one's own. But from that fairly strong reference to it there, one is tempted to wonder whether at the end the feeling of incongruity between his talents and training on the one hand and his station in life on the other was catching up to him, and leaving him with a sense of failure at the end. If so, it may have been a failure he had come to terms with at least in part by seeing that a certain eeriness of circumstance had made it so. It should come as no surprise if that feeling of failure was growing stronger at that time. They were the most depressive years of his life. He had given himself so completely for so much that seemed to be good that even that strong spirit had to be showing signs of being very tired. For many years by then he had had to scratch out a meager existence by going about peddling his books of poetry. The ten-acre farm, where once the tasks had virtually all been handled by the children, now became his sole responsibility, and he was trapped between his own inability to keep up with it and the sense that to sell it would have seemed like signing his own death-warrant. The printing press, one of his major joys, for which once his sons' quick hands had set the type, now waited idly for his no longer nimble fingers. Even the churches, as he confides to his diary, whose warm reception of him and what he had to say had been a constant lift to his spirit, seemed no longer interested in him, and that added to his feeling of having been discarded before he was ready to be. The long talks with my mother as they waited for their first cup of coffee to heat up at five in the morning turned more and more inward. And then the incongruity between his dreams and talents and the Dakota that was to be his destined arena stood out and seemed to slide over into the question, "Where did it all go wrong?"

But despite whatever that evidence may be worth, it is countered by more telling things. Of these the largest is that at the end of his life he did not go out a-whimpering, lacerating himself with his failures. His last years showed a mellowing of spirit that put him on top of things, happily at peace with what his life had been and where it had been lived. Whatever sense of incongruity there may have been between talent and reward at least by then had given way to the fairer images of completion which he cherished, to the sense of having "fought the good fight." In an eloquent phrase he once used in speaking of a friend who had died, he died "a Tennyson death," in the spirit of at least *Crossing the Bar*. The image of the Arab nomad (and my father would not have missed the appropriateness of that term for himself) who "folded his tents and quietly stole away," or of him who "gathered the curtains of his couch about him and lay down to pleasant dreams"—these fitted his spirit at the end, not that image of having thrown his life away on nowhere.

But now with all of that out of the way, we can and have to start all over in the telling of the Dakota story. As to how it came about that he got there there are no mysteries. He got there because he had no other options. He knew nothing about the place, and had never been there, and it was by his own testimony the last place in the world where he would have chosen to go. Vocational opportunities, in the church as in education, were scarce; neither was at the time particularly what one would call a growth industry. And he surmised that he might have narrowed his own range of possibilities even further simply by having taken the year to attend Yale; people in general, he thought, might have been wondering in consequence of that act just how serious he was about the ministry. The fact simply is that he went to Dakota because there was no other place to go.

But that does invite a little speculation. Could not, should not, my father have been at least a bit more energetic and imaginative and competent in enlarging the number of his options? There is no way of knowing how aggressive he may have been in seeking out opportunities for himself. From his own character and temperament, one must infer that he had been fairly passive about that. Aggressive as he was in mastering an environment once it was given to him and in that to express and rise to self-reliance, that aggressiveness certainly was never translated into an equal aggressiveness in opening doors for himself. As a "job-hunter" I think he must be judged to have been quite inept. Maybe his Calvinism got in the way, in so far as that might be taken to mean that in energetic job-hunting one would run the risk of "running ahead of God." Calvinists were just not of a mind to do that. Or could it have been his sense of being "special"? After all, in a just world, the special person should find the world beating a pathway to his door. It would be unseemly to be out looking for that world. And to add to that, people around him had apparently some vague intimation of that "being special"; waiting for the great opportunities they supposed were destined to come to him got in the way of their offering opportunities he would have been only too glad to get.

And another speculation: had some "larger" opportunity opened could he have handled it—a respectably established parish, for instance? I do have a few doubts, and would keep them to myself, were it not for the fact of his fairly early exit, at least partly at his own initiative, from the parish setting, which does point to some lack of fitness, whether of ability or disposition. If being a parish minister was simply confined to the preaching hour (two hours was more like it then) then, yes. Well, at least later, his competences did not seem to be confined to that. In the one-on-one ministering to the sick and the sorrowing, at least in

The Golden Age

later years, there was a kind of magic touch. I recall going with him on some rounds, and even at a tender age I had some sense that when he walked into a newly-bereft home his sheer presence, much more than anything he said, seemed to have the effect of a benediction. But that may have come only with the process of growing more mature and acquiring a reputation as being one who deeply cared for people. I have to think that "ministering to the spiritual needs of the sick" was an art that did not come easy to him. Nor, from everything we later knew, would he have inspired great confidence in himself as an administrator of an institution, nor did he exhibit much interest in that. Neither did the idea of "converting" people seem to be a natural part of his make-up, but I shall have to come back to that; so far as I know he never seemed to have articulated this for himself, but it is hard to come away from a look at how he did approach persons without a feeling that he was not disposed to do anything but show them what they could become; but I may have to modify that. But when you take away all of those elements from a parish which seemed to be his weaker points so far as both interest and competence went, there was not that much left, even by the simpler ecclesiastical standards of seventy-five years ago.

But what if the doors had opened more than they did to entrance into the academic profession, even the occupancy of a major university chair such as did form a favorite content of such fantasies as he built up over the years? In that, I have no doubt, he could have managed and managed brilliantly, more so than in a parish situation. That would have put him in not only the habitat that would have been natural for him, but also one, (particularly by so much as the university might approximate his favorite image of it, the proverbial "Mark Hopkins on one end of the log and the student on the other") in which he would have truly revelled. He certainly would have been more excellent as a university professor than as the farmer or bank teller he once toyed with becoming.

But none of all that happened. The fact is that there he was in Dakota and that story is the one that must be told. The main point of that story must be that everything about it belies the image of it being a matter, in his own mind, of throwing his life away on nowhere. The image of that being on the order of a "Siberian exile" was there, and when it did pop up it troubled him. But so was another cheerier image, of an Abraham answering the divine call to leave what he had thought was his place in the world and to go out, not knowing what he might be getting himself into, but in faith. The "land of promise" part may have been a little slower in coming but it, too, was to come. Whether manfully or spontaneously it was the Abraham image which finally obliterated the Siberian one.

For one thing, the quality of the people with whom his lot was cast stood as a rebuttal of the image of "throwing his life away on nobodies." They simply did not fit the "dumb farmer" cliche. It is not a little astonishing to note to what degree our own American mythology about what we are and our image of the immigrant have simply made us blind to what, at least in important part, was the fact of the matter. We do carry the image of social and cultural mobility as a special virtue of the American story, but we imagine that all mobility has to be upward. We never seem able quite to see that there can be or was in some circumstances a mobility downward. Hence the quick assumption that if one were a farmer now he had to have been a serf yesterday, when maybe at least as probably today's farmer had been yesterday's landed gentry. Or we may be trapped by the immortal inscription on the Statue of Liberty pleading, "Give me your tired and your poor"—trapped into believing that if one were an immigrant he had to have been tired and poor. Certainly as likely as not the immigrants turned out to be the specially endowed, the imaginative, the able, who because they were not about to lie down and play the helpless victims of their places and their times became the trailblazers toward better things. The founding fathers, to name some, were not the beaten ones, the ignorant louts, the ones who could not make it. They at least were the people of the larger hope, with competences to realize it. The story is certainly as diverse as the number of the people and the places from which they came. I do not know what generalization might best fit the Dutch immigrants, but it is as certain as that they came that at least many brought huge talents and aggressiveness and the drive not merely to escape adversity but to turn whatever successes they already knew into larger ones.

And the people who helped to people the western plans were surely a case in point, and another image must be uncovered than the more common one which they were saddled with. The fact is that the behavior of the climate on which so much depended for the success of their agriculture turned out to be not as steadily propitious even as the one they left behind and that as a result they were not generally prosperous. If anything, and in an at least proximate though sweeping generalization, they may have stood a notch taller than their country-folk who had peopled western Michigan. Those had been at least relatively poorer on the average, and were hampered by that in the range of options as to where they could go. Above all they needed forests for their lumber with which to build homes and industries, and forests and great soil do not necessarily go hand in hand. The settlers of Iowa, and from that the Dakotas, in contrast were wealthier ones, able therefore to have *their* lumber shipped up the Mississippi and thence overland. Though greater affluence is no guarantee of higher culture, there is at least some basis for a theory that a century later the difference still shows, in the relatively more spontaneous participation of the Iowa Dutch in the full search for all the good things which together make a cultured life. Such also were those who had moved on to the Dakotas. They proved to be an intelligent and receptive folk to whom my intellect-oriented father never needed to talk down. Not all of them but some of them by my own recollection were simply people of all around competence and culture, enough of them to set the dominant tone. The parents of one of my later faculty colleagues who originated in that area were simply aristocrats in every sense of the term but the conventional one. So what, if my grandfather was a wealthy landowner, of the landed gentry, measuring life by how little there was to do? My grandmother at any rate, through some fine instinct and necessity, produced in at least some of her progeny a different breed of aristocrat—who measured life rather in terms of how much could be accomplished, how much they might enrich their world. And if life was harder in Dakota, by adding a healthy dose of hardihood, of sharing freely one another' setbacks, of an uncomplaining patience—in all this, as my father came to see, the Dakota people easily put their more prosperous countrymen across the Floyd to shame, in their inner personal strengths.

Years later my father was to tell with enormous relish the story of a fellow minister in Dakota, who, when he received sympathy from his former classmates in New York for having to live "so far away," replied with the telling put-down, "From what?" In venturing into South Dakota, of which, as he says, he knew nothing, so could have had no large expectations that he would find in Dakota what he found, but he surely found it and was exhilarated by it.

But discovering, or seeing afresh, the good quality of the people with whom his lot was cast is not the last word, and the picture of my father would be left distorted if I were to leave it there. For it would leave him standing there simply as an "elitist" (in today's damning term), one only conditionally interested in people: as long as they were hard-working, good students, moral, and interested in the ideas which he came to share with them. Before he was done with Dakota something important was to happen to how he looked at people, and it happened mainly, I think, because of or under the influence of the Dakota experience. That this did not come as naturally as did Academe, I infer not from the absence of an active concern for the underprivileged but from the fact that he always seemed to be surprised to find this concern in himself. The Frisia memoir had made reference to how freely he mingled with the children who came from less-advantaged backgrounds than his own. One does not talk that way unless one is conscious that he has done this, and by so much as one is conscious of it it is a disposition that does not come spontaneously. But if that spontaneity is, by however little, missing from his childhood days, it caught up with him, without his having to plan it or work for it, in Dakota. For what emerged, as some of his poetry along with the still-living recollections of those who knew him make clear, was eventually an interest in persons which was unconditional. If he liked Dakota people first because they were able, he got to liking them simply because they were people. That they were *able* catered, after all, to his professional instincts as a teacher and preacher; that each, no matter how humble or how much "a failure," was a person, catered to an instinct which, no matter how academic he might pride himself on being, ran at least as deep as that, his *human* instinct.

But all of that was only one part of the equation that was supposed to make up the damnation, "He threw his life away." The other was the job he had. The time of the completion of his education coincided with the time when the Dakotans had finally decided to establish an Academy (secondary school) for the education of their youth, and were hesitating only because of uncertainty as to whether they could find the resources to pay a staff. The site was to be in Harrison, which, when our family lived there in the twenties, consisted of a loose cluster of some thirty or so homes. The reason for the location, I suppose, is that it was located within the easiest reach of the largest number of prospective students. The village, small though it was, also boasted both a Reformed Church and a Christian Reformed Church, and this was to be in some way a joint venture between the two Dutch constituencies.

The pieces of the puzzle came together when it was discovered that the Reformed Church in Platte, a larger town twenty miles away, and too small to be able to support its own full-time minister, was interested in finding someone who could give weekend services there. So the arrangement was made with my father, and he made his move to Dakota at the beginning of September in 1902, and certainly not without enormous misgivings. And if it was not quite what he may have privately dreamed of as his professional milieu, it certainly was more than he would have allowed himself to hope for, and even more certainly more than he could ever have brought himself to ask for. Indeed, if one can get past the distorted judgments which our cliches about success trap us into making, it is hard to imagine a more ideal situation for a person of his make-up to have gotten into.

For one thing, it was just about the only kind of situation he could have ridden into with his bipolarity intact. Everything points to the fact that that bipolarity of interests was there, at least from sometime during his college days when his professional directions took shape. He was, as his late memoir says it, "above all a good servant of Jesus Christ." and apparently equally, "above all, a scholar." He was of the seminary but equally of Yale. He was as much Athens as he was Jerusalem and Jerusalem as much as he was Athens. And here in Dakota, a world appropriate to him was handed to him on a silver platter, and in a pioneer form which made it pliable to his interests and ingenuities. He would not now, as he was obviously reluctant to, have to make the fateful choice between them, a choice which would have necessitated lopping off one part of him to be left to wither. And the feeling of pride in knowing that there were not many persons who by training and disposition were as fitted to occupy the dual role as he did not go unnoticed by him. And as if to make the situation even more ideal, each of the two parts separately was handed to him in a form which could hardly have been more suited to his exact taste than if he had had the planning of it.

So he was a week-end preacher. And those Saturdays and Sundays were packed full of challenge and fulfillment. What confining his parish work to week-ends said to him was not that he could feel at ease, knowing that he could in good conscience expect to be forgiven if some of the parish work was neglected. In accepting the appointment to the parish he thought of himself as having committed himself to do whatever would be done by a full-time minister, even though he accepted only half the salary they offered. What it did mean is that he was free to zero in on what were the real concerns of a parish ministry, and free as few are to battle against having to get tangled up in the frittering kinds of things which organized churches get themselves involved in and which he deplored. Sunday he was free to get to what was to him the heart of the matter, the preaching (twice, for at least close to an hour for each sermon) and teaching in the Sunday School. And Saturdays were just as packed full of what came at first less naturally to him but which by being diligent about it he acquired a talent for and an interest in, the one-on-one standing next to people to their troubled times, sickness, bereavement, failure, a hailed-out crop, a barn burned down in the prairie-fires which were the scourge of the Dakota area. These all were the core of a ministry, and it was a boon to him that as a week-end preacher he was free to stick to the core.

And the Monday through Friday assignment at the Academy came in a no-less challenging and for him glorious form, given his own natural instincts for judging values in education and the general values of the community. This was, to be sure, no Yale, but it was an *Academy*, and whether in a quixotic moment or with a twinkle in his eye or in dead seriousness, before he was done with it he called the Academy the "Harvard of the West." (I have no idea how Harvard sneaked into the label and not Yale!) He had, after all, been doing some school teaching for a term or a year here and there, but it was elementary school. And he had loved that, nor was there ever on his part any trace of condescension toward that. Now to be teaching in the Academy was clearly a step up from that, even for him, who was not thus wholly free from the conventional image which says that to move from elementary school to secondary school (and to college and to graduate school) does represent a step upward. But that it was an Academy rather than a "mere" high school meant as much as that it was a secondary school. Not only for him but in the eyes of the community generally an Academy meant a special quality that a high school could not equal. For one thing, it had the image of being more rigorous in its intellectual discipline. An Academy's student body bore the image of being of special quality, whether there was a selectivity about who might enter, or whether after the fact they *became* special under the stimulation of the image that by virtue of being in an Academy they were marked off as being an elite. My father was not bashful about extolling the virtues of the Academy, nor was this simply done under the pressure of some need to do promotional work. One recent correspondent remembers how my father got involved in (unresolved) debates about the relative merits of the Academy and of the South Dakota State Normal School forty miles away.

Given all of this, my father's anxieties about what he might be getting himself into when he went out into that Nowhere of Dakota were quickly allayed. He had to have at least some feeling that he had "never had it so good," if not the feeling that nowhere else could he have had it so good.

But there is more to the story than I have so far told, to both parts of it, the Platte part of it and the Harrison part of it. There was more to the Platte story than that it was simply a preaching location where he could nourish his preaching instincts and his deeply humanitarian concerns. It lay in the nature of the town itself, which in fact bore an image which no one who had not lived there could find it easy to associate with Dakota, and way back at the turn of the century it was a particularly unlikely image if one remembers that the Dakota territory had been divided and achieved statehood only a couple of decades or so earlier. Where Harrison, that tiny crossroads village, was an ethnically pure community whose life centered about the tilling of the soil and the life of the church (and with the coming of the Academy, the educational process) Platte was something else. And if the Academy and the parish gave free reign to my father's bi-polar professional interests, the village and the town fed another kind of bipolar interest. There is every indication that he felt himself as much at home in the one as in the other.

No conventional image about life in the northern plains at the turn of the century would quite fit Platte. It certainly was no roaring, wide-open frontier town, nor was it an area rallying point for deprived and beaten pioneers scrabbling a precarious existence out of an always stingy nature. Even more certainly, it was no Sioux Center, and save for that very special breed that would see in Sioux Center a new Zion, it would by general consensus be a much more interesting place—and I am sure that even my father had that feeling about it. It did not know anything about elite urbanity, but it was not a nothing-town either. By my father's account, every western European ethnic group from Norway to Italy and including Switzerland was represented in its population (which, in the Middle West, of course, always includes not only those who live within the town's limits but all whom the town serves and profits from as the market area). And everybody seemed caught up in the race to put their ethnicity behind them and be stirred together in the melting pot—except the Dutch, and even among them, if their surnames by any stretch permitted them to be credible about it, their self-designation as French Huguenots took precedence over their being Dutch.

Nor was it, in at least one meaning, a godless town. It could boast churches representing seven or eight mainline communions, including Roman Catholic, plus a few not so mainline ones. Among these the Dutch, as has been their story and is to this day in the Middle West, stood out as special if not by the quality of their piety then at least by their visibility in their being strict sabbatarians, driving in what my father called "a parade of carriages" to church on Sunday, and always for both a morning and afternoon worship service. My father seems to have felt quite comfortable with his fellow-clergy, especially with the resident Catholic father, and comments with a twinkling detachment on the interesting clash between the priest's ready habit of moving from the confessional to enjoy his beer and back again, and the Methodist preacher down the street ranting against the evils of demon rum even in that mild form.

Hermit-like and ascetic though he sometimes describes himself as being, my father found the people obviously very interesting. No cringing fuddy-duddies, those. One maybe serious, maybe slightly askew, entrepreneur took one look at some incredible cabbage heads in a garden and leaped in an instant to the dream of filling up the whole area with cabbage farms, making Platte the sauerkraut capital of the world with himself the head of a giant sauerkraut factory—financed, no less, by his fellow-Baptist, John D. Rockefeller. The big thing in fact was the raising of beef cattle, different both from Iowa and Wyoming in that they could in Platte have the best of both possible worlds, the wide open ranges where the cattle could be raised toward marketability for almost nothing and then their own produced feed grains and feeding lots where they could "finish" them for market. My father's glowing account of the size of this operation strikes me as being a little overdramatized, but I do have strong nostalgic recollections of joining friends and riding the ranges from dawn to dusk in April, checking out the number and condition of new-born calves which seemed to be occupying every imaginable little sheltered cranny. The railroad that had by then been laid as far as Platte was not for nothing. The local banks were putting a million dollars a year (an incredible sum when fifty or sixty dollars a month was a good livelihood) into financing of the operations. And I can believe it, remembering that, though each year's prospects were unpredictable chiefly because the searing southwest winds of the summer dog days could ruin everything, when things were good in South Dakota they were very, very good, and when they were bad they were very, very bad.

Nor were the people all content to be the local yokels. My father meant to be saying something about the people in general in describing with particular relish the exploits and reputation of one "Cyclone Jones" (maybe a fictitious name in the novel), a local rancher, who won his title not on the ranch but in the state legislature by his robust and generally maverick proposals. I think he was even trying to tell us something positive, this time about the depth of living among the common people, when he pointed out the town's "hermit", old man Carlson with a long flowing white beard, who in his younger years had built a large and beautiful home to which he expected to bring his bride; but when she jilted him at the last minute, he built a tiny shanty next to the mansion and lived in that for the rest of his days, with, so the saying went in the community, no one's ever having set foot in the mansion. And my father reports his especially high esteem for the quality of the women in the community; one needs to be only a little bit careless to be caught up in the impression that every last one of them had originally come out from the eastern schools to be teachers. And would you believe a "Shakespearean Society" in town?

"Throwing his life away on nowhere"? The *Arabia Deserta* image simply does not fit how he talks about Dakota. I have to make a judgment that it was "worldly" Platte as much as "godly" Harrison (and maybe Harrison as much as Platte) that accounts for my father's not just contented acceptance of Dakota but his sense of deep-rootedness in it. When time came to pull up his roots he had to leave a very big part of himself behind. And I am fully persuaded that he would never have left it had not the editorial post he was later to occupy opened and in the same year in which his eldest son was ready for college, which was the same year in which the Northwestern Academy in Orange City became a Junior College—all of which he welcomed, but less because it did mean getting back to the Sioux County that had nourished him than because this opened the door to his fulfillment of another major passion, to see all of his children through a college education. I never heard him use the expression but I am willing to wager that it crossed his mind, "If you want to know me, you have to know Dakota."

The work at the Academy in Harrison for those four years from 1902 to 1906 is in its way a very different story than the Platte one, but is quite as remarkable in itself. That career occupied his week from Monday through Friday. And his commitment to this was no less than his commitment to the church. He went at his dual vocation with a vow to himself that he would do no less at both its parts than if each was a full-time job, even though for each he let himself accept only what amounted to half-pay. In fact, his readiness to serve the parish for five hundred dollars a year caused some consternation among his clerical peers, who took pains to go on record as insisting that the fact that he would serve for half-salary should not be construed to be a precedent for other churches in their determining what salaries they should pay their ministers.

The Academy venture was most unusual in almost every respect. For whatever reason, the initial commitment called for taking in twenty students at the beginning and then simply seeing these through the four years without admitting a new class in each of the following years. It is plausible to interpret that action as being taken to avoid getting into a longe-range commitment from which it might be uncomfortable to extricate themselves in the event that the financial support should fail. These twenty who were taken in obviously represented an accumulated backlog of people who were bent on an education but for whom there had been no opportunity until then. And the group of twenty did remain virtually intact throughout the four years.

That the planners of the Academy had full confidence in my father's competence and judgment is evidenced by the fact that it was left wholly up to him to determine the curriculum and really the whole tempo of the program. But the determination of the curriculum was not very complicated, for my father simply went into that with a vow that the students in the Academy would come out with no less than if they had attended the well-established Academy in Orange City. The curriculum included Language (Rhetoric, Composition, and Survey of English and American Literature), Latin (Ceasar, Cicero, and Virgil), Greek (Xenophon, the Iliad, and John's Gospel), History (a survey of Western History plus English History) and Physics and Botany. And the discipline was rigorous, as rigorous for himself as for the students, since he would not have been able to live with himself had he compromised or allowed the students to. Classes met throughout the morning (with a daily chapel service for good measure), with assignments given that would guarantee the students would be working solidly for the afternoon and into the night. These students were generally older and more mature and self-disciplined than the average high school student even in those times. He could capitalize on their obvious zest for learning. Even so, he did encounter a student strike! This was incredible for those times and even more incredible given this highly select group of students. But he responded to the strike not by easing up on the load but intensifying it. The record does not indicate clearly whether this was done overtly, by announcing his response to the strike, or subtly, by tightening up without their realizing it, but the probability was that it was the former, since he draws an analogy between his response and that of Pharaoh when the Hebrew slaves complained about the impossible rigor of their brick-making tasks. And he apparently had the backing of the student's parents in this, for they were driven by the typical immigrants' passion to obtain the very best possible education for their children.

But the pay-off was to come. There are no exact figures as to how many of the twenty went on to college, but it is clear that most of them did. And none who applied for admission to college had any difficulty in getting in—they were simply accepted and no questions asked. The memoirs say that some went on to be teachers, one became a doctor, another a lawyer, there was a minister and an engineer and a professor. Of these I can reasonably confidently identify only the professor, who not only became a professor but by general consensus just about the most outstanding professor in at least the twentieth century history (to this day) of the strong college where he spent his career.

The travelling that this dual professional assignment entailed is a quite incredible saga of its own. A good twenty miles separates Harrison and Platte, and at that time the church was located somewhere southwest of Platte, and my father speaks of a trip of nearly thirty miles. My father's proud boast was that never once in those four years did he miss or come late for his Saturday morning responsibilities in Platte or his eight o'clock Monday responsibilities in Harrison. Roads were scarcely more than ruts worn into the prairies by buggies that occasionally travelled between the two towns. But to appreciate the magnitude of the achievement of never having missed an appointment one has to know something about Dakota blizzards and cold. Forty degrees below zero was not uncommon and sustained cold spells in which the temperature did not rise above twenty below zero for two or three weeks were expected when winter came. Nor was it uncommon for people to freeze to death, sometimes within a few hundred feet of their homes, when the driving blizzard simply wiped out everything that one might use as a clue to where he was. Once my father was totally lost, as the ponies somehow headed north when they should have headed east, and when finally late at night he came upon an isolated farm house he found that he was farther from his destination than when he had started out. After warming up he headed out into the blizzard at midnight and arrived in Harrison in the small hours of the night. "The show must go on!"

That one episode dictated switching from buggy to horseback as his means for getting back and forth. For this he equipped himself with a combination of overcoats and blankets which together were so cumbersome that once mounted on the trusty steed he did not dare to get off for fear he might not be able to get back on, and one kindly farm lady en route got into the habit of watching for his coming, whereupon she would run out with some hot coffee and warm food to serve him as he sat on his horse. Through it all, he was sustained by Kant's "du sollst!" and Emerson's, "When duty whispers low, 'Thou must!', the youth replies, 'I can!' " Well, not wholly by that; he did allow himself the fleeting fantasy that someday someone might erect in his honour, somewhere along the route, an equestrian statue to commemorate this quite incredible feat!

And as if all that was not enough to fill up his days (and nights) it appears that those same years marked the beginning of his output of poetry. This information rests on a somewhat precarious base because it seems never to have occurred to him to put a date on anything. There did appear among his papers small bundles of sheets of poems, just about equally distributed among Dutch, Frisian, and English. From the appearance and recognizable antiquity of the envelopes into which these bundles of poems were stuffed, it does appear that they may have disappeared into those envelopes at a very early date. The handwriting, which was to deteriorate somewhat under the mad writing pressures of the editorial days, was uniformly at its meticulous best. But most importantly, scattered here and there among the sheaves of sheets there is a poem written on the clean side of a slit-open used postal envelope which bears the cancellation date—and some of these are dated 1902 and 1903. There is, in the papers I had access to, no evidence of any other kinds of writing. This is at best a thin bit of evidence on which to base confident inferences, but it at least suggests that a lot of poetry writing was crowded into those already crowded times and also that his first form of written articulation on a sustained scale was poetry, of which there was to be much more in later days. Not only that, but as compared to the later poetry which was relatively heavy and didactic in its own way, that earliest poetry does show up as being in somewhat lighter vein—which may be evidence of a certain exuberant joy at being at whatever he was busy with.

Try as I may, I cannot escape the feeling that to my father those four years marked, in his own retrospect, the highwater mark of his whole professional career. I have to rely on the fact that he never wrote about any episode in that career with quite the unmitigated enthusiasm that characterized his recollections of those years and their sense of satisfying achievement, satisfying both in view of what he accomplished and in view of the sheer impossibility of it all and the unswerving commitment he brought to doing what had to be done.

How it came about that the four-year assignment to this dual responsibility was terminated, I simply have no way of knowing. This remains a mystery about my father. In a way, it generally does become reasonably clear how he got into whatever in his life he got into. That was clearly not by his designing, or with any clear consciousness that at any given point this or that kind of enterprise seemed like a good next step to take toward fulfilling some articulate life ambition. Though his thoughts about things were wholly from within, and even the kind of person he was was determined by himself, what particular assignments he got caught up in were not of his determination. It was simply a matter of a fundamental and simple opportunism—at certain junctures this or that became available to him and there were no other options in sight.

But as to how whatever he got into came to an end, this remains mostly a mystery. Suddenly what was there simply was not there any longer. It is not that the Academy folded after the four years. I do not know whether there were gaps in its history along the way; if so, they might well have been avoided had he stayed with it. But at least after him others took on the work of the Academy. It is not clear whether his connection with the Academy was terminated at his initiative or at someone else's. Though he did in his ensuing assignment express some feeling of relief that the arduousness of the four years was behind him, he soon become once more involved in another dual responsibility which could not have been much lighter than the one he left. I have no way of knowing whether, in the event we could know how his various "jobs" came to an end, this would prove to be an embarrassment or arouse the feeling that on occasion he was quite unjustly dealt with.

The only speculation I can offer as to why the arrangment in this case was terminated comes by way of interpolating into it something which I know he was to encounter later. And this is worth mentioning in some detail because I think it may go far toward explaining why, as far as his professional life was concerned, he always had rough going. This revolves around the notion of "image" and "substance." As far as substance is concerned there is no doubt that he was producing, in both his dual capacities. As far as his work in the parish was concerned, that it was being satisfactorily done is best attested to by the fact that in the middle of the four-year span, he was finally ordained to the Christian ministry and formally made the minister of the church in Platte (where up to that time he had carried out the responsibilities simply on a contract basis—possibly more oral than written). And as far as the quality of his performance in the Academy was concerned, the record simply spoke for itself.

But there was the other matter, of how the operation looked. It certainly did not have the appearance of being a first-class operation. And while my father never in his life could bring himself to care how operations might look (quality of achievement alone mattered) the sponsors of the Academy, I think, may have viewed things differently. They were not nobodies, with no sense for how things should look in order to look respectable. And the Academy surely looked like the proverbial one-horse (no pun intended) operation. Pride in appearance was possibly important to the sponsors along with pride in substance. This simply is as much a fact of life for any would-be significant operation as is the less overt pride in substantive quality. That would have to be taken in large part on faith in the people who are the key performers. Even my father's refusal to accept as much salary as he could have had entered into the picture. It is hard to avoid reading that otherwise than as evidence of a person's low estimate of himself; and if one has a low estimate of himself it is hard to avoid receiving a low estimate from others. And the answer to that is never as simple as my father seemed to make it, in his pervasive insistence that it is quality alone that counts while appearance has nothing to do with the matter.

At any rate the four years did come to an end, and I come back to the judgment that in retrospect they were his proudest and most satisfying years. Not even his later five-year stint (from 1923 to 1928) at the Academy, and this time with that as his whole responsibility, could elicit the same enthusiasm on his part. In part that had to be the result of a new policy, which there was no way of avoiding, of admitting a Freshman class every year. On this basis, this simply became, if not impossible then certainly a far less rewarding context in which to work. Each class was tiny, ranging as I recall from maybe four to seven students. And though from those years there also emerged a steady trickle of persons who went on to prove themselves and the Academy by their subsequent professional successes, the daily routine had to be broken up, at least in theory, into four times as many little segments. This had to result in a sense of scatteredness in the enterprise which compared unfavourably with the earlier stint.

Immediately following the four golden years of his career my father became, presumably, the full-time minister of the Platte church, a position he was to hold until 1912. During those years things did move forward, at least apparently so. As far as his general circumstances were concerned they had improved, and relatively he seems to have been better off than probably at any other time in his life. Probably with what he had been able to save during those years in which, as he suggests, he lived frugally not wholly because he had to but because he was so engulfed in his work that he had no time not to live frugally, he was able to purchase sixteen acres of land on the outskirts of Platte. To own land, as I have pointed out, was not just economically important, though it surely was that. It was a crucial move toward achieving economic self-sufficiency, which he always strove with incredible ingenuity to attain. To say that he reached a point where there had to be a cash outlay only for sugar and salt and postage stamps is an exaggeration but not by much. Owning a piece of the earth was, beyond this, a kind of "spiritual necessity" for him, or to use a term which for a while in this century we have kicked around quite freely without knowing exactly what it

The Golden Age

meant (but it sounded impressive) this had "existential" significance. Without land one really could not feel himself to be a complete being.

But those years in the parish, by his own account, were in a couple of ways uncomfortable for him. Surely by his judgment more than by the judgment of others, he began to have some doubts about the quality of his preaching. He began to wonder whether possibly he was importing too much of his purely intellectual interests into the pulpit, and to wonder whether with what he brought he was really reaching his audience or talking to their interests and needs. He also confesses in retrospect to having felt quite ill at east over the fact that he was after all a bachelor occupying a sensitive position for which a bachelor was ordinarily not quite acceptable because not quite trusted. He was not insensitive to how easily the most commonplace and open and honest and well-intentioned behavior in relation to the women members of the parish might be read by the suspicious in the community as an overstepping of the bounds of proper decorum and purity.

Whether his anxiety about these two things was warranted is another question, and I have to rely on what is there to rely on in venturing a couple of reflections. As for the second, given his self-confessed shyness in the presence of women and his commitment to rigorous moral self-discipline, it is at least plausible to suggest that his anxiety about whether he was behaving properly was simply a natural corollary of his intense wish to be in every way above any possible reproach. There *is* reason to believe that only the intensely moral can worry about whether they are being moral enough, just as it is typically the intensely religious who worry about the adequacy of their religious commitments.

As for his wondering about the adequacy of his preaching, there is evidence that the one thing that explicitly triggered his discomfort was the fact that occasionally a parishioner would slip him, whether innocently or in order to be telling him something, an evangelistic religious tract. It is given to relatively few preachers to be so self-confident about their own preaching that receipt of religious tracts would not be read as a subtle form of criticism, and the more conscientious the preacher the more likely it is that he will see it as critical, rather than as simply one person as a matter of casual interest passing a tract along to someone else.

Against the possibility that there might have been a gratuitous and critical motive in handing him the tracts, I can only set the other evidence which I have, that among all whom I knew who remembered him in longer or shorter perspective, one thing they seem to have remembered him for was that his preaching was unqualifiedly interesting and uplifting. These unsought testimonies seemed so spontaneous that to say of my father as it was said of Jesus, that "the common people heard him gladly" does not seem irreverent.

One does not naturally turn to a preacher's ten-year-old son for any kind of objective judgment on the preacher's competence, but I do have some recollections, for whatever they may be worth. This was later, in the twenties, but on occasion I did accompany my father on some of his preaching missions to near-by villages or country parishes. I have a clear recollection that on such occasions even I noticed that the parishioners did not fall asleep in church when my father was the preacher. This was something new to me. It could have been because my father had the advantage of being a novel figure, as compared to the practice when he was not there. Some of these parishes were too poor to be able to afford the services of a resident minister, but the church services were held regularly, with one of the elders simply reading a sermon from the books of sermons with which every church was amply supplied. "Preeklezen" (sermon-reading) was the name for it. These performances, though by people of good intent, and though dutifully attended, were obviously hardly calculated to be inspiring. This was simply a generally accepted characterization. But even where there were resident ministers, much of the preaching tended to be heavily cliched. I have clear recollections of sitting in church and inwardly playing the irreverent little game of trying to stay two or three sentences ahead of the preacher—and being quite proud of my high batting average. That kind of preaching was itself quite conducive to putting people to sleep. But the blame could not all fall on the preacher. Farmers who had put a great deal of hard physical labor into six long days a week would naturally find it a bit difficult to sit still for upwards of an hour and a half without dozing off. And it got to be quite accepted that after "the preliminaries" of the worship orders and when the sermon was about to begin, the men-folk would slip off quickly into sound sleep, while their anxious women-folk kept devoutly hoping that they would be able to guess when the next loud snore might erupt, so they could beat it with a hopefully unnoticed nudge in the ribs. And another little game we played, privately of course, was to guess how many of the elders, who occupied raised pews in the front of the church and half-facing the congregation, might drop off to sleep on this particular day. But the point of this is that, as I remember noticing, when my father was the preacher people did not fall asleep. But then again, remembering that despite his small statue he had acquired a public image as a rather formidable person, maybe no one dared to.

The reference to the four years of dual service at the Academy at Harrison and the parish at Platte being the highwater mark of his professional career needs a bit of refining. Simply left there it could be invidious, as a suggestion that he may have been somewhat less than wholehearted about his later undertakings or that his later declarations of his satisfaction in what he was doing were not quite honest. I hope this does not begin to slice things too thinly, but a refinement here is important for what it says about my father. There is a difference between a spontaneous involvement in something, getting involved in something to which one is led by his affective instincts, and an involvement which comes about by a willed commitment to it, in this case an involvement which was not less total for its being basically a willed one. The difference between the golden four years and what came later is that those four years belonged to the former, the others (with the possible exception of the later years as editor) belonged to the latter. The difference is a little harder to defend, even though I have no doubts about it, when one considers that my father found so much emotional satisfaction in throwing himself wholly into what he had accepted as his duty, that he very probably could not have been aware of the distinction between doing what he spontaneously wanted to be engaged in and what he understood to be his duty. Both were, in the last analysis, deeply satisfying, but the satisfactions were significantly different from each other.

V
Variations on a Theme

But the years I have identified as the high-water mark of his professional career were such not merely because they were the best fulfillment of what I have called his affective instincts. They were also the years in which he finally achieved his self-definition, in the sense that during those years more than any others he became set in the mold in which he was to live out the rest of his life. But since, if one is to speak of his coming to be defined, he was defined as much by his participation in the life of the parish as by the life of the Academy (and vice versa), I cannot cut those four years off from the next six years after he had left the work of the Academy and became, in a loose manner of speaking (as the sequel must show) and professionally speaking, simply the minister of a parish. That begins to sound as if I am forgetting the earlier reference to his being an inwardly determined person and switching to the contrary image of his having been defined by the accidents of his circumstances. The fact is that he was an inwardly determined person, but he was not determined in a vacuum. He did chuckle over the story of the man who went about boasting that he was a self-made man, to which the irreverent wag replied "Good! that surely gets the good Lord off the hook!" But the fact is that his being what he made himself is something not only that he has to bear but would have been proud to bear. Even his long struggle with economic hardship, we suspect, was not wholly imposed on him but as much, and fairly proudly, a condition which he created for himself.

That the four years of which I have spoken were the years which were most crucial in his becoming what he was is not all that remarkable. The ten years from 1902 when he began his dual ministry to 1912 when he terminated his connection with the parish in Platte were, after all, the years between his thirty-first and forty-first birthdays. And though dramatic changes can happen in what a person is after forty, they surely are more the exception than the rule.

But there certainly is nothing simple about the effort to encapsulate what by the time of his fortieth birthday he was. Theories about this flow easily, but so soon as one gets one of them down on paper it wants

Variations on a Theme 65

to fall apart and must be either scrapped or refined. So the next must be said very carefully.

The first thing that I am reasonably confident of is that during those years his Christian commitment was both strengthened and stabilized. This is to take nothing away from the sincerity of his commitment first made in college days. But when one has one foot in Athens and another in Jerusalem, it is hard to avoid having these work against each other. The academic scholar's inherent impulses are qualitatively different from those which typically move the Christian preacher, and even the valiant medieval scholastic efforts to remove the tension do not quite come off. But during the ten years the Christian (or, better, the Christianizing) impulse did grow stronger, not so as to negate the academic impulse but so as to make that impulse serve the religious end.

Early in those decisive years, there is evidence that he was not clear whether academe was a means to a religious end or the converse. Good Christians have the kind of personal traits of deep commitment, self-discipline, and devotion to duty that make good students. Yet this seems to be gradually overshadowed by the conviction that one becomes a good scholar so as to become a good Christian. It was by way of "capturing the university" that America, in his view as it emerged in these years, could be Christianized (though quite inconsistently with this and perhaps only by way of paying his tribute to the power of music, he was also known to have said, "You can have the people's schools if you will let me write the people's hymns"). But the strongest evidence that he got around to seeing education not as an end in itself but as a means to the Christianization of culture comes in the enthusiasm with which he asserts, in reference to the Academy curriculum for which he had responsibility, that finally the most important episode in the daily schedule was the chapel service, "the capstone of learning." While it is also clear that he never got involved in thinking through the tough issues involved in the attempt to hold intellectual integrity and devotion to piety together, there was no doubt as to where his instincts lay, even though it is also clear that he had no inclination to let those instincts undergird any form of clericalism, as in effect, if not always by intention, they had in the Medieval mode of thought. He speaks of himself as being irreducibly "a missionary at heart"; and while that never seems to have been associated with any kind of dramatic conversion or effort at converting people, it did mean a changing from one set of commitments to another. This growing definiteness of Christian commitment is also evidenced by the fact that, to the extent that the old fantasy, if it was such, of sometime having an opportunity to occupy a professorate in a prestigious university was alive, it had shifted from the prestigious university to a seminary, and one certainly hears no more about the dream of teaching mathematics; now it is teaching Hebrew. The only reason for the otherwise somewhat puzzling termination of his ministry in the Platte parish was that he had designs to go back to complete a doctorate, but now in Hebrew language and literature, as an appropriate vehicle by which to enhance the Christian ministry.

This coming to definiteness in his Christian commitments does not appear to have been due to any kind of dramatic or subtle Christian experience. There did linger in his mind his mother's hope that he might become a Christian minister. One has to speculate that it may have been due to the fact that, as a professional minister, one does assume a commitment to sustaining and promoting Christian commitments in others. By accepting the image of this as what ministers are expected to do, one works his way into this as a gradually habitual set of mind. But I have an additional explanation which by my judgment in retrospect may have been an even larger factor. He did, clearly and strongly, indentify himself in a way and on a certain level, with the Dakota people. And in one way or another, their deep piety rubbed off on him; or more affirmatively, he could not but see how much piety meant to them especially as they had to confront their hardships.

For whatever reason, that Christian commitment was to bear his uniquely personal stamp and did grow stronger and remain permanent. For one example, in his later years as editor, the writing of a weekly exposition of "The Sunday School Lesson" was clearly as much at the center of his interests as was the writing of his hefty editorials on many topics. This kind of Christian commitment was not, as it can become, a hope that somebody else out there will commit himself; it is but a reflection of a powerful commitment which he at the end was ready to claim for himself, when he said, "I have tried only to be a good servant of Jesus Christ." Much of what he was later to come out "against," generally to the dismay of his fellow-clergy (like his opposition to the church's provision of pensions for its ministers) can be understood only as that seems to be a reflection of his own commitment, which to him meant that no one was to achieve personal gain (or maybe even personal comfort!) from being a minister. To do so actually did or ran the risk of compromising the commitment.

The second item in the "profile" of what my father settled into being during those years of his formation I mention now because it is one of the simpler and surer items. It is his commitment to Dakota, and that means a commitment to the physical land(!) and to its people—so that it is sometimes hard to know which he is talking about when he talks about his love for Dakota. Again one ostensible factor in his decision to resign his position as minister of the Platte church was his hope of being able to go back to graduate school. There is no evidence that, despite the definiteness of the resignation, any of the usual initiatives had been taken looking to admission to graduate school, nor is there any indication as to what graduate school he might have had in mind to attend. What is recorded in his autobiographical materials is that when he did face up to the imminent prospect of leaving Dakota, he simply could not bring himself to pull up the now deep roots and leave.

Explicitly, the fact that he now did own his own piece of God's earth there had something to do with it. And I have already mentioned the kind of deep meaning that owning land had to him. But knowing his general disposition toward Dakota, there has to be more than that involved. It had to include a deep affection for and commitment to the people who lived there. Though he went to Dakota in the first place without any great enthusiasm and even with some misgivings, once he had gotten there and lived with these people, he developed a rather overwhelming sense that they were indeed *his* people, by both affection and commitment. He obviously felt completely at home with them, as he never had or would among any others. And the bonds had grown tighter because he had shared not only their joys but their hardships and sorrows.

One needs to bring to this account only a trace of cynicism to suspect that maybe what really proved to be decisive was not so much an affection for the people there as a kind of reluctance to put himself in a new and strange and therefore scary environment. There was enough shyness in his personal make-up to reinforce that, and by that much his decision to remain in Dakota would certainly lose some of its aura.

On this as on numerous items in his life story, it *is* possible to engage in a ready psychoanalyzing of his actions. In his case as in everyone's, one can look for such psychological explanations, and one can always with a good deal of confidence psychoanalyze someone into innocuousness or oblivion. That option is as clearly open to us as is the other option of taking his life and thought at its face value and let it say what it can. But the two options are not equally open to a son writing about his father. I have neither a warrant nor a wish to erase the meaningfulness of his relation to the Dakota people by arguing that the commitment was made only to save him from the anxieties that might be involved in having to enter and adjust to another environment.

But, as I have suggested, it was a commitment to the land—to this particular land—as much as, or inseparably from, a commitment to the people. That kind of mystical bond to phsyical land is hard to appreciate for any who have not had the experience of it, and if we can appreciate it at all we would more naturally associate that kind of bond with something like the awesomeness of the Swiss Alps or with Germany's Black Forest with its many moods. But these were simply plains. Again it is hard for anyone who has not lived in and identified with a farming community to have any sense of how life is tied up with the land. My father was aware of and himself fully shared in the Russian peasants' mystical (there is no other word for it) affinity for the land. For him and for the devout of Dakota this issued in a deep sense that one's relation to the land defines his relation to God—though not merely as if this is a nice poetic analogy. When one's life depends on it there is not much time for poetry. My father's sense of this ran so deep that he would, I think, have been willing to say that the relation to the land is *one with* the relation to God, bringing together the warm outpourings of gratitude for good times but at the same time, in that relatively unpredictable region, never taking the good times for granted.

The third item in the profile of what I think my father settled into being has to begin by picking up the earlier reference, in talking about his boyhood days in Friesland, to his consciousness of being a "special person," a person "set apart." Something important happened to what that was to mean, not, I think, by a self-conscious design but as he acted on his instincts. What that tended to mean earlier, and was to remain as an occasional whiff of dreaming, was that some day from somewhere there would be handed to him a position in which his very considerable intellectual talent would have opportunity to express itself fully. What now happened to that, and especially in the "golden years" of his dual professional responsibility, was something very different. From being associated with the dream of a dramatically special thing to do, it was gradually transmuted into meaning that he had to do whatever there was to be done in a dramatically special way, like never missing a Saturday morning or Monday morning assignment, no matter what the circumstances might be.

I have only one small cue which would indicate that he was not wholly unconscious of this. As I was working my way through his papers, I picked up one day a chaotic handful of miscellaneous papers, and a tiny newspaper clipping (obviously a newspaperman's "filler") fluttered to the floor. He did a fair amount of such clipping, and to us who knew him there never needed to be any puzzlement as to what was going through his mind as he clipped it. This contained some lines from Robert Louis Stevenson:

The best things are nearest; breath in your nostrils, light in your eyes, flowers at your feet, duties at your hand, the path of God just before you. Then do not grasp at the stars but do life's plain common work as it comes, certain that daily duties and daily bread are the sweetest things of life.

What doing whatever was there to be done in a special way meant at least was that it should be done perfectly. But this perfectionism did not mean what it more commonly means, a hesitancy about turning something out until it had been amended to say exactly what he had in mind to say. There is no evidence that in his writing (save for the poems) he ever went over things to change or correct what had flowed from his facile pen. What the perfectionist instinct meant was that he would throw himself completely into whatever he was doing so that he worked with an intensity that was quite exceptional and over and above the call of duty. Nor did he have to force himself into such exertion; it was as natural as writing or teaching itself, and this brought him to a strong feeling of satisfaction with what he had done—he had given himself wholly to it. That much of his specialness is, however, not so unusual in a professional.

There was, I think, something else involved which did set him apart. It was that everything was also done with a sense of moral compulsion. The sense of perfectionism was not measured at the end by how perfect the product was, but by the amount of sheer dedicated energy that had gone into it, and by how much the effort had cost him. There was a kind of monastic self-denial involved, and it is not trivial to say that by his judgment nothing was well done unless in some way it had been done under difficulties, whether the difficulties were inherent in the undertaking or of his own making. This is the kind of thing that prompted some of us in the family to say, only half in jest, "If there is a hard way to do something, he will find it," and "the hard way is always the better way," for it seemed to him that it was the difficulty of doing something that added a certain moral quality to the effort.

My father was not wholly insensitive to the possibility that to ordinary people he may have seemed somewhat "strange" in how he went about things. To the extent that this might have been so, this strangeness was clearly not a planned one; it was I think predominantly a not surprising consequence of his instinct for finding his own specialness not in what he did but in how he did it.

The fourth and final item in this profile of what he had become must also begin with a sense of his specialness, his "set-apartness." It is certainly merely to say the same thing in synonymous language to say that involved on his part a sense of detachment, of being aloof from what was going on around him—not, I hasten to add and emphatically, an aloofness of unconcernedness or of cool detachment. It was rather the aloofness which meant a refusal to submerge himself in existing beliefs and structures and institutions, which left him free always to sit in critical judgment on them and to become, in a label that fit and pleased him, the "gadfly." But it takes an extraordinary sanctity to keep that image from shading off into the quite different image of "I against the world," and to keep that one from shading off into the still quite different image of "the world against me." All of this did not at all mean a failure or refusal to identity with persons in their joys and their sorrows. If it is possible to sustain this distinction, it did mean a refusal to identify with people's accepted beliefs, their mores, or the directions in which they may have wanted to move. Again I must mention his "inwardly determined character." It left him with a basic inability and/or refusal to let himself become really a part of the world in which he lived.

How far this extended and that it was at least in part a cultivated disengagement from the life around him are both exemplified in an unlikely circumstance. Though he was a theologian by profession, I do not remember ever seeing a book on anything even resembling theology on his bookshelves or ever seeing him read a theology book. He was later to write on some theological concerns, but they like everything else came from inside. And though he was, after all, a professional clergyman with a deep interest in the Bible, he took great pride in not only not having the usual array of biblical commentaries but in never having used one. He tells of one squirming moment when a travelling book salesman came to town selling a set of commentaries, only to be met by my father's protestation that he could not afford such an expenditure (somehow he overlooked what usually he would do in such a case, add to it a stern lecture on the evils of relying on biblical commentaries). Not to be daunted, the salesman left but was back in an hour having persuaded one of the elders of the church to buy the commentaries for my father. There is no information about how he may have squirmed out of that one, but I am sure that somehow he did.

Though a deeply interested scholar, my father had clearly no feeling for what Jacques Barzun was to say in his classic, *The House of Intellect*, how scholarship is more or less formally a corporate enterprise to which many contribute their bits and in which one person's beliefs and understandings are given an opportunity to be critically examined and amended by many minds. And equally, my father had no living sense of the dimension of the church's existence as an organic entity developing through time, the product of the accumulated insights and wisdoms

Variations on a Theme

(plus the not-so-wise increments) of many persons over a long time. That he missed this carried enormous liabilities with it—he might have benefitted from having tossed his ideas into the arena of open debate and critical examination.

This quite deliberate preservation of his detachment from his world resulted in his closing his eyes to something else. That is that in reflection we do not merely constantly build stronger and stronger cases for a particular commitment; any position must also defend itself against alternative possibilities. For him there seem never to have been alternative possibilities. And he was able to indulge in the luxury of seeing every issue in simple black-and-white terms. There may somewhere be a heaven of black and white, but in this vale of tears it is more correct to say that we are doomed to make our way more painfully, torn this way and that by the rival pulls of various options neither of which is wholly good or wholly without merit.

But this detachment had its gains, too. It meant that in what emerged from him there were no second-handed contents, no hand-me-down beliefs, and he was free simply to say what he said with the deep conviction which he arrived at after long and careful brooding over it in his own inner sanctum. And maybe that habit of detachment also spared him some risk of frittering away his energies on the trivia of side issues.

So, all in all, he would surely fit into the term, "a loner," with at least some of the many kinds of things which that term covers being especially apt in describing him. In no sense, I think, did the term mean for him that he was drifting off into simply a welter of private rambling musings on irrelevancies. Though he did not and could not submerge himself into the world around him, he never forgot that it was the real world around him that mattered. His concerns were the concerns that did or should trouble his world. And if he did, so to speak, speak from inside his private cave, the voice that came out, though not an oracle's voice, was consistently a prodding, provocative voice, combing the power of a voice of conscience with the power of a voice that was "intelligibly intelligent." He may have struck some people as being "strange," even "odd," but that, I think it fair to say, was overshadowed by the other fact that when he spoke they knew they had to listen, either with their consciences or with the better wisdom of their common sense.

That image of not being able or willing to identify with the world in which he lived is, however, belied by evidence that in regard to some and maybe many particular items, he did seem simply to have adopted his community's mores, so far as they involved beliefs or standards of living. By so much as that is true, however, the community's beliefs he identified with were the beliefs of a community that had been shaped more by its Christian beliefs than by anything else, so far as conscious shaping was concerned. So that if we must have the picture of him as sitting in critical judgment on the modes of his world's life, that would mean sitting in judgment on "the world" from inside the sanctum of the Christian-shaped community, again, in so far as that shaping was non-explicit and non-overt. There is no doubt that that note is there. But by my judgment that dimension of casting a critical eye on all he surveyed takes a fairly remote second place to another domain of judgment. This was a sitting in critical judgment on the very community some of whose mores-beliefs he had made his own. That is getting pretty close to sounding paradoxical, but I think there is nothing paradoxical about it. It does call for some refining.

My father did accept at least a number of specific items contained in the mores, but where on the average they might have been accepted simply because they were the acceptable thing, my father generally seemed to come up with a better reason for accepting them. He was able to see something in the conventional belief that people did not conventionally see in it, to shoot for what may have been an authentic dimension in it as against some drab, repressive, commonplace meaning.

This has to be seen in some concrete exemplifications. For one such example, he, like the Christian-influenced community around him, strongly objected to "the movies," which along with dancing and card-playing came close to being identified as the three cardinal sins. And he was not above seeing these as most folks at least said they did, as being inventions of the devil. But when he reflected on the matter, something very different emerged—not merely a different reason for objecting to them, but a very different image of what kind of experience seeing a movie might be. And those even of his younger conservative friends for whom his objection to movies was going too far were, I think, never able to understand this. Though I guess never in his life did he see a movie (had he, he might have liked the experience, because he was in a way an open individual) he at least knew that there one relied on "seeing something." But he was also clear that seeing a movie compared quite unfavourably with what one stood to get from the experience of reading a book. From where he saw it, the old saying about a picture being worth a thousand words simply was not so. A good literary description of, for example, a hobo would yield a much richer image of the hobo than a picture could, or perhaps even than meeting a real-life hobo. For in both the latter cases, so little detail would really be consciously attended to, and such as there might be would be superficial, because in observation of a picture the mind is simply an inert observer, while in relation to a literary description the mind is forced to be active in moving beyond the words to attain a mental image. He was firmly convinced that reading Shakespeare was a richer aesthetic experience than seeing Shakespeare could ever be. That at least is by no means implausible.

At the risk of belabouring the example, however, it would be misleading if I simply stopped with the image of his having better reasons for a belief than other people did, even when he believed the same thing that they did. The next is important because it says something of major importance about the exact character of my father's intellectualism. If one were to ask what was his *actual* reason for his views on movies, the fact that the belief was part of the mores of his community or his analysis of the literary experience, the answer certainly is not a very clear one. If I had to answer it, I think I would have to say it was really because it was part of the mores.

I think it was the philosopher F. H. Bradley who, in a moment of for him unwonted cynicism, spoke of philosophy as finding bad reasons for what we believe on instinct. Change the wording from "bad reasons" to "good reasons" and you will have a pretty good description of my father's intellectualism. His "reasoning" was not a process by means of which he went about determining what belief he would hold. That was settled by "instinct", or, in this case, an equally immediate, non-discursive acceptance of a belief because it was included in the mores. The reasoning came afterwards, not so much as a way of strengthening his own belief (one strengthened one's belief only by strengthening one's commitment to it) but as a way of persuading others. And it is exactly in this kind of context that he did his most creative thinking.

The example of the movies is but one among many others in which, though he accepted many of the items in his community's ideology, he was able, in the above sense, to give beliefs a more authentic foundation. He did accept his community's sabbatarianism but at the same time did not accept the common image of that as meaning that one should spend that day in a lot of busyness about going to church two or three times, nor in putting much energy into reading and meditating on peculiarly pious items. It was a time to let the mind do a little resting, of gaining a surcease from the burdens of toil, of giving oneself time to breathe, something that for him (Hebrew-like) began of a Saturday evening. He accepted the devotion to the Bible as the community's mores did, but with a vast difference. To my knowledge, he did not get involved in the conventional busy concern about whether or not the Bible was inspired.

To him that issue receded into a pale second place in comparison with the authentic experience (which was very real to him) of finding it inspiring. He accepted, and for himself, the community's emphasis on winning converts to Christ. But this was never simply a matter of moving from not being a member of a church to being one, and dramatic conversions seem not to have held any interest for him. Conversion meant rather a moving from one quality of the inward life to another, maybe one which consisted of inner peace in the presence of hardship, but more clearly one which consisted of firmer moral commitments and inward discipline.

Such, I judge, is the correct profile of what my father settled down to being, by a process that may have had its roots earlier in his life, but reached its apex in the first ten Dakota years. And I can think of nothing that might indicate that there were later important deviations from it, even though he was to move now and then in some fairly different orbits. There were a couple of substantive additions but no significant deviations.

I have spoken of those first ten years in Dakota, the first four in his dual role as educator and minister, the last six as parish minster. But in the process of getting on to the description of the years and of what my father became in those years, I had to delay reference to a very different and indeed quite puzzling part of the activities of the last six years of the ten.

There, too, we find a dual role. While he was the apparent "full-time minister" of the parish, he also got involved in what were equally apparently "full-time" responsibilities in education—but this time in public education. How this came about or what prompted this is not clear. It is even less clear what if any official arrangements were entered into, especially with the parish, to make this possible or acceptable. But where information is lacking one can at least do some speculating (so long as it tries to be responsible) triggered by a general image of what kind of person my father was.

One such speculation begins with the fact that he was by instinct the eternal educator, and it was hard to keep him out of that. Another looks to the fact of his boundless energy. With the most conscientious will in the world, it would be hard to conceive of the work of so small a parish as being a fulltime job in the sense that it would use up his energies on a daily or weekly basis. And he certainly had no mind to see himself as occupying a leisurely, sinecure position. He would certainly have lost sleep over that. There is some indication that economic necessity may have had a hand in this, though as far as I can uncover, there was a salary connected with the parish responsibility which should have been reasonably adequate to meet the demands of a person with his simple and disciplined tastes. But there is reason to believe that the contractual figure for the salary was one thing and the actually paid salary was another. Yet no one involved would even toy with the notion of breach of contract. The church could be confident that it had conscientiously done the best it could. And my father would be the first to trust that it had. After all, times could be very hard for the Dakota farmers, and my father was so much with them in their hardships that he would be quicker than they in being satisfied with their contractual shortcomings.

There is, indeed, an explicit reference to the economic difficulties that, in a moment that is as completely out of character as any I know in my father, points out that he did allow himself to think, maybe not without a tinge of wistfulness, that a publicly supported institution, like the school, was a whole lot more sure from an economic perspective than a privately supported institution, like the church. One has to wonder, in reading such scanty information as is available about that episode in public education whether he may not for once in his life have grown so weary of the constant struggle for an economic security that seemed always to elude his grasp that he was tempted to scrap much of what he had come to stand for and to cast his lot with the greater stability of position and income that the public schools seemed to afford.

In a way, it is true, it is not so astonishing that he would have turned again to teaching, no matter on what level. He had, after all, had by this time some experience in public school teaching. And though that certainly did not offer all that he had dreamed life might offer him, he had obviously found a good deal of satisfaction in the steady routines of teaching. It is fairly certain that he had not himself sought out the teaching position that now opened to him; the vacancy seemed to be there, and he was one person who was available to fill it. But though that is true, he had had by that time the experience of teaching those select students in the Academy, and while he was engaged in that the public school seemed lame by comparison.

It *is* clear that he did not, during those public school days, surrender any of his conviction that education should be permeated by religiousness. Surprisingly to us who suppose that the question of Bible-reading and prayer in the public schools arose only much later, in what has been referred to as the post-Christian era of American life, that issue was very much alive even then, and even in a small rural town which, with its several churches, was presumably pretty solidly Christian in one sense or another. True, Madeline Murray O'Hare had not yet been invented, and opposition to Bible reading in the public schools was not of secular inspiration. It was mainly the Roman Catholics who raised the question of its appropriateness, even though my father speaks of being on very good terms with the local father.

But he had his own way of handling the issue. He tells in retrospect, and not without a trace of glee in the telling, how he managed to get past the opposition, as quite without their realizing it and certainly without their being able to do much about it, he managed to sneak a good dose of religion into the daily routines. It was done in a manner that the Supreme Court in all of its later decisions regarding religion in the schools would have found quite to its liking. At that time my father had already developed his habit of doing a good deal of memorization. While teaching at the Academy, he reports, the daily history lesson was always memorized. And in the public school he memorized and recited a good deal of poetry for his classes, presumably the literature classes. But there was nothing to prevent him, as he recited the poetry, from throwing in, unannounced, a good deal of biblical citation. So he did have the satisfaction of getting the pupils exposed to a fair amount of the biblical literature.

Most surprising about the public school episode in his career is the fact that he was not only there as teacher. He became also involved in the administration, and seems to have been even rather heavily involved in the politics of the schools, which seems to have gotten quite messy at one point. The principal came under local fire for some reason and the usual process of the community's taking sides for and against him happened there. As nearly as I can make out from the sketchy details, my father may have been in an ambiguous position. Had the principal been ousted, as some wished, my father might have been in line to assume the principalship. But at some public urging he also ran for a position on the school board, on the apparent assumption that if elected his would be one more vote in support of the retention of the principal. He lost the election by the narrowest of margins (a single vote), and when the smoke of battle had cleared, he found himself in the position of assistant principal.

Nor did his involvement in the schools stop there. In another out of character episode, he soon ended up as the deputy county superintendent of schools. This involved, by his account, the responsibility for inspecting a hundred and fifty schools. That sounds like a lot of schools for a fairly sparsely settled area so the figure is hard to believe, except for the fact that these were the days of the one-room country school and these had to be built so as to provide reasonable access by walking to all the children of the county.

Again, one is at something of a loss to account for how that public school excursion came to an end. The indication is that it ended also in 1912 at the time of the resignation from the parish, which was, by his report, a resignation by mutual agreement and in good spirits all around. And if the parish resignation was prompted by a desire to return to the university, then that may also have prompted the termination of the school connection. But at any rate, there he was, as he says, back at the same point he had been ten years earlier, and again having to do a good deal of worrying about what he would do next.

VI
God's Greyhound

But as usual, something else did turn up. I do not think my father was of that pious temper which would believe that when the doors were all closed, all one had to do was pray hard and like some miraculous manna from heaven something would turn up. But he could have had that feeling after the fact this time. For a vacancy did occur and opportunely he was available.

The regional governing body of the Reformed Church, the Classis, did fairly regularly employ someone in the capacity of "classical missionary," whose responsibility covered the whole geographical region of the classis, which in that case was pretty extensive, ranging over the whole of South Dakota except for a strip nearer the Iowa border, up into North Dakota, and, I think, down into Nebraska. He referred to this as his "far-flung empire," though it certainly was much more far-flung than empire. He grew to extend the affection he had developed for one particular spot of South Dakota to include at least corners of North Dakota and Nebraska. The latter was summed up in a poem entitled, "The Sandhills of Nebraska."

The job-description included responsibilities for general supervision of existing parishes and the launching of new ones. He did, as I shall note further along, operate on the assumption that the Reformed Church should remain available to Dutch people wherever a cluster of them, no matter how small, was to be found. But the establishing of parishes had been pretty well taken care of before his time.

The one church, so far as I know, which he did have a hand in developing was the church at Strasbourg in North Dakota, the town whose later claim to fame was that it gave Lawrence Welk to the world. And Strasbourg holds a special place in my own recollections because my father was stranded there in a March blizzard the day I was born, and for many years scarcely a birthday passed without a reminder in his birthday letter that that had been the case. (Incidentally, this little item lifts the curtain on the fact that over the years my father was away from home a great deal, and as a result many of the responsibilities of the family had to be borne by my mother alone.) The circumstances of the founding of the Strasbourg church were highly unusual, and serve to illustrate the extent to which my father was willing to go in pursuit of the interest of particular individuals even if it meant moving counter to the dictates of the community mores. For the details of this I must rely on a couple of somewhat disconnected items and I hope that the story that emerges is a correct one. Some of the details were told me many years later by a friend whose origins lay in Strasbourg. According to the story, one of the fairly prominent members of the community was living under a kind of cloud. He had immigrated from the Netherlands, where he had left a wife and at least some children, presumably with the understanding that he would send for them as soon as he had established himself in the New World and circumstances made it possible. But the plans did not quite work out that way. Instead the man fell in love with a lady in the community, who moved in with him as his common-law wife, by whom he then had a second family. Other than that irregularity, the indications are that he and his family were generally recognizable as "good people" in the community. But this did put serious restraints on his participation in the life of the church. Not only so, but there seemed to be some difference of opinion in the community, as to whether he should be simply accepted by the community or whether in view of his past those restrictions, unofficial though they were, should be maintained. The founding of the Strasbourg church, according to my informant, had something to do with all of this. I have to guess that, since the man in question did play a role in the life of that church, the Strasbourg church was founded, probably among other reasons, as a place where he would be fully accepted. And the story does not end there. Years later my father was to write a novelette (I hand-set the type for it!) based on the story of that family. His hope, as he expressed it to me, was that when this was read by the man involved, it would move him and his wife to proceed, however belatedly, to sanctify their marriage by going through the traditional Christian marriage rites. (I have no idea how the issue of possible bigamy was going to be handled.)

With the exception of the Strasbourg church, the work of the classical missionary consisted rather in meeting the religious needs of the existing and widely-scattered parishes. Several of these were too small and impoverished to support their own minister—*ever*, since the Dutch were also very clannish and there was no prospect that the churches would ever grow much beyond the size they had by then attained. Regular Sunday worship services were held, but generally under lay leadership, including the reading of a sermon by one of the elders. A few times during the year my father would visit these parishes, which in some cases consisted of no more than a dozen or so families. (But since families of twelve and more children were not uncommon, that could still add up to a sizable number of people.) The pattern then was for my father's visits to span two week-ends, with the week between being devoted to visiting each of the families and taking care of such situations as might call for pastoral strengthening and encouragement. (This meant that during those six or seven years he was away from home a great deal and that, along with the fact that by the time he began raising his own family he was near forty so that there was an unusually large generation gap, prompts one of my brothers to reflect that the family was raised primarily by my mother.) But on these visits to the various parishes there was a lot of catching up to do. There was always the observance of the sacrament of the Lord's Supper. There were confirmation services to be taken care of, and always a number of babies to be baptized, catechetical instruction to be carried on, and marriages to perform. They were very, very busy times.

Travel arrangements were of course difficult, and it required a great deal of ingenuity to arrange rail connections to each place, at least close enough to them so that he could be met at the train station by some member of the church and brought to where he had to be. In the process he spent many a night sleeping on the hard benches of some railroad depot waiting for the next day's train to come along. The difficulty of getting where he had to be, coupled with the fact that this very home-loving man had to be away from home so much, should have been enough to make those years some of his least happy ones.

But actually, they did loom in his recollections as some of his proudest years, not because he was doing the thing that he would have chosen with any kind of spontaneity, but because he was able to commit himself wholeheartedly to it and by the sheer strength of that commitment to make the arduous responsibility satisfying.

It was in these circumstances that he preempted for himself the title "God's Greyhound." The title was not original with or for him. It had been used first to apply to a predecessor in the classical missionary post, who by his own tirelessness in carrying out the responsibilities had pretty much created the existing specifications for the position. I do not doubt that it was the fact of the label he could apply to himself as he handled these responsibilities that made it easier for my father to get excited about the job. How large these years loomed in his recollections of his life is indicated by the fact that when in the late forties he wrote the "novel" which was "the true story of his life," he chose to title it, "God's Greyhound"—which nothing in the story really fits except the experience as the classical missionary.

But there is more to this story than meets the eye. There was in fact a quite complex inner working for all of this, without which we would miss a good deal of at least one facet of my father's make-up.

For one thing, there was the obvious churchliness aspect. I have mentioned and will have occasion to mention again the fact that my father did have more problems with churchliness than with the Christianity which was its reason for being. I have to believe that it was precisely during those missionary years of his life that his sense of church was stronger and livelier than at any other time, including the years during which he had been a parish minister. The latter could slip, after all, into a kind of routineness, with the accompanying need to stir things up and keep them genuine. This did not come naturally to my father. But on his visits to the various isolated parishes, he appears to have been impressed by how much religious beliefs actually meant in the lives of sometimes hard-pressed people. He spoke proudly during those years of the fact that he was indeed a "missionary," whose function it was, obviously, to bring the unchurched into the church, to retain people for the church, and to raise the quality of their courage in meeting the hardships of life and of their commitment to behaving as good Christians should.

Besides that he acquired a deepened sense of what it meant to be a "pioneer." His home base in Platte was close enough to the edge of the developing of the West to give him a sense of pioneering even there, but it was not quite pioneer country even so. Indians, so much a part of the pioneer days image, were part even of the Platte scene, and I have at least a dim recollection of groups of them coming to set up an overnight encampment on one corner of our homestead, on the edge of town. But these had already accumulated some of the accoutrements of civilization in that they travelled about in small caravans of the white man's wagons, mainly as an occasional spillover from the Rosebud reservation which lay to the West across the Missouri, and thus they lost a good deal of the romantic associations with which the existing mythology surrounded them. But my father had more primitive associations with them out in the more westerly regions of Dakota. He loved in later years to regale us with the story of the day he had visited an Indian settlement and shared a meal at which the participants ladled their food out of a common pot. When his turn came he was admonished to, "dig deep; skunk in the bottom." It was in his experience of these relatively more pioneering areas that he was able to recapture the pioneer's sense of isolation. But in his experience of these more pioneering folk what seems to have appealed to him was not the restlessness which by the conventional image drove the pioneers further and further westward in fulfillment of a manifest destiny which would not permit them to stop until they had reached the edge, the Pacific. The Dutch pioneers were different. They rode westward not under the lure of the unknown, as I have mentioned, but on the quality of the soil. What impressed my father most about them was the still glowing sense of self-reliance of the people. This he found it easy to identify with, and it was this as much as anything that made him so completely at home among them.

But there was more. There are many incidental items in the surviving papers that make it clear that during these years his own ethnic sense, which had always lurked somewhere on the fringes, received a new emphasis. He had never apologized for being Dutch even though even then the Dutch were the butt of many not very complimentary jokes, much as, for example, the Poles were in later times. He was obviously saddened by the eagerness of at least some of the Dutch to obscure their ethnic identity. And the sense of ethnic pride was to loom large, later during his days as editor of the Dutch language weekly newspaper. One of its unannounced missions, as he saw it, was to serve as a center and rallying point for the preservation of the ethnic identity. And at least at that time it was the Dutch ethnicity that seemed natural as over against the Frisian, to which he was to give a flurry of attention. For a time in the early forties, when he was without fixed assignment of any kind, he flirted with the notion of producing his own publication. He lacked the resources to turn this into a steady affair or to develop any kind of stable means of distribution. But the title he gave the few issues that were sporadically produced was "Ons Volk" ("Our People") and confesses that he finds a strong pull toward the notion. That ethnic, sense, I judge, was much intensified during his missionary years.

But this, like so many items which he adopted more or less as part of the existing mores, bore its own personal stamp, and was really a quite sophisticated kind of ethnocentricity. It ran very deep and quite unselfconsciously. Indeed, for him the ethnic tie and the sense of the bond of a common religious faith were so closely intertwined as to be quite inseparable, as is so largely the case in the historic manifestations of a strong ethnic sense. "Irish" or "Catholic" seem instantly to suggest each other. We never have settled the question whether "Jew" is a religious or ethnic (or national or racial) designation. In the particular focus of his "greyhound days," "Dutch" and "Reformed" may have blurred together, as appropriate synonyms for each other.

Still, where I suppose the usual association of the ethnic sense is with a feeling of exclusion of the non-ethnics, there was none of this in his consciousness, if that meant a sense of Dutch superiority, or a sense of having to build fortress walls around this identity to protect it from the world. No one would be turned away from my father's church because of race, color, or creed. He was simply and deeply and honestly and unpremeditatedly interested in people for what they were. He had an abiding sense of being able to learn something from everybody by learning about them. Nor was he only conditionally interested in them, seeing them as only possible candidates for conversion. This kind of authentic interest in persons for their own sakes is one of my abiding recollections of him in his associations with people. The ethnic diversity of the Platte community was a stimulus to him. He was deeply interested in "Uncle Billy," a local brain-damaged character of uncertain origin, and at Billy's death wrote a touching ode to Billy, "the hero of the hoe." He tried to get next to the old hermit Carlson, of whom I made mention above. Difficult as his own economic circumstances were, he and my mother adopted in every sense except the legal one a young Italian boy who was working on the railroad maintenance gang. In those days, a Mr. Dooley, then the headmaster of a school for black people in Alabama, made a regular tour of the churches to solicit financial support. Mr. Dooley (it was always "Mr.") was the blackest of the black and his visits to our home on those occasions were major events. And there was Mr. Hofer, the German giant who was spiritual leader of a communal religious group (of, I think, Doukhobours) which occupied an unbelievably pastoral "saucer" which erosion had carved out of the flat lands of Dakota, and I remember the awe I felt as the German language flowed fast and furiously as if there was never enough time to complete the mutual communication which each sought with the other. Years later my father met in our home a Chinese student, the first Chinese he had ever met, and he was simply elated by the opportunity through him to "know what 400,000,000 Chinese were like," quite overlooking the fact that Stan was a purely Anglicized product of the British educational system in Hong Kong. These are the things I remember which are my basis for saying that his ethnic sense was not at all associated with any feelings of exclusivism.

But there was a strong ethnic sense even so. And in a loose way of identifying it, it was the sense that though no one could be excluded from his church or the circles of his friends, all Dutch were to be included. This manifested itself in the strong sense that wherever there was even a tiny cluster of Dutch people, they should have access to a Dutch church. This was later to run afoul of an understandable anxiety of the denominational leadership about the wisdom of a policy which called for pouring sustaining funds into these tiny outposts. That leadership did have to wrestle with the always tough question of how best to make responsible use of always limited financial resources. But to my father, any move in the direction of curtailing support for the tiny churches that were scattered over the plains could be read only as a betrayal by the church of its own. And that not because "Dutch was better." It was rather because a person's life could not be whole unless it included a strong sense of identity with other persons, an identity which could only be realistic in terms of an identity with a people that had a historic identity. He had a powerful sense, and in this he certainly was not alone, of how life would be impoverished by a loss of the sense of ethnic roots, which was constantly threatened by the counter-slogan of "America the melting-pot." That this insight on his part showed a good deal of prescience is certainly indicated by the enormous root-hungriness that followed the appearance of Haley's *Roots* in our time.

But even this was not the whole package. Again he developed a strong sense of identity with the sometimes individually isolated Dutch family. From the perspective of the New York offices of the church, out of sight could mean out of mind. But this could not be the case for my father who was out there with them. This is dramatized by one particular instance which loomed large enough in his consciousness to warrant his later writing a fairly extensive memoir describing the experience. His record as missionary was again virtually impeccable in so far as his never missing a connection for an appointment was concerned. But once he did, whether because the trains simply did not run on that day on their normal schedule or because he had made some mistake in planning his trip connections. For whatever reason, he did miss an appointment, arriving somewhere in the general area of where he was supposed to be. Driven by a very bad conscience, so the memoir reports, he began walking, somewhat vaguely, in search of someone whom he knew lived somewhere in the area, but apparently too distressed by the failure to make his connections he walked and walked, until finally as the day wore on and more by chance than by design he spied the place he was looking for. That lost Sunday, so he reports, was somewhat redeemed at the end, because he had been able to speak to this very isolated family about the possibility of becoming identified once more with the church which they had deserted. Standing close to the isolated ones he had a rare ability to put himself in the shoes of the forsaken ones, and the word "lost" acquired a very concrete, though almost physical meaning. Then he saw his role as that of the biblical shepherd who left the ninety nine sheep who were safely in the fold to go and search for the one that was lost. Though I am not sure that kind of hunting is what greyhounds are particularly noted for, that did not really matter. It comes closest to what the label meant in his adopting it for himself.

But this missionary episode also came to an end, and this event of leaving an assignment is at least by his own account less puzzling than most. These were the war years, and during those years he had at least started on the road of pacifist protest against war which was to play such a large role in shaping his circumstances for the next decade. And by his estimate of the situation it was quite because of his pacifism that the pressures against his continuation in his missionary role began to build. There is no other evidence that this was or was not the whole reason for the eventual termination of the appointment. The story of his pacifism looms large enough both in his thought and in the shaping of his circumstances to deserve a separate analysis. I introduce it here only insofar as it was, apparently to the best of his knowledge, the reason for the failure to continue him in the greyhound role.

So again, there he was, driven to looking for something to do. And again something fortuitously appeared. It was back to teaching once more, but this time under different auspices and in an environment that was more congenial to him than public education could ever be. He became a teacher in the local parochial school sponsored by the Christian Reformed people of the community but not without considerable backing from the Reformed churches which mainly throughout the denomination had not been particularly parochial school minded. In that kind of environment he at least did not have to smuggle in his religious interests in education. The years from 1919 to 1922 were thus stable once more, and he was free to be at home with his now growing family. And during those years the school flourished, as is evidenced by the fact that it was able to extend its program beyond the elementary level into the high school. This was the first time that my father seems to have been strongly committed to the program of parochial education, which differed at least in the degree of consciousness of being a closed, self-protective society even from the image of his earlier academy. He was to be a staunch advocate of the parochial school from that time on.

And yet the image did not seem wholly to fit his temper, since, naturally inquisitive as he was about everything, it did not come easily to him to have to pose as the authoritarian, the indoctrinator into right beliefs and the warder off of wrong beliefs. He did have some sense of "the secular world" being headed off in some wrong directions. But, for one thing, this was a corollary of his own self-image as a prophetic-minded critic of the world in which he lived. For another, as a later look at some of the positions he took as editor will make clear, the judgments he expressed were not judgments which he passed on the secular directions just because they were secular—which, I assume, *is* the temper of the parochial mind. They were the result of two things. One was his cherishing of the traditional values, like the value of home life as that could be realized in rural America and of the farmers' economic independence. The other was his wisdom in foreseeing that if secularism should persist in the directions it was beginning to take there would be major headaches ahead for the world. There was a strain in him which seemed to insist that the truth was well able to take care of itself without having to have extraneous walls of defense built around it, as in parochialism.

Nor, as one might expect by now of anything that my father committed himself to, was his commitment to parochial education the simple thing that it seemed to be for most, simply the execution of a mandate to preserve the purity of a community which claimed to have the truth. Here again, the issue grew more complicated until it is hard to say which of at least two major impulses was mainly determinative of his parochial commitment. Looming at least as large as any defensive impulse to preserve the purity of the minds of the young was his insistence on, in one sense, "free" education. He clearly carried over into his educational philosophy from his Netherlands background the sense of the "free church" as against the "state church". Neither religion nor education were, by his judgment, the proper function of the state. He had the sense to realize and to fear the extent to which a public education under governmental control could become a most powerful instrument by means of which the state could exercise a tyrannical control over its citizens. Nazi Germany and Marxist Russia were to come along later as prize exhibits which substantiated those fears. He had also some sense that a public educational system would inevitably tend to become monolithic, to impose a sameness of ideas nationwide. To him the inevitable form that that would take would be for the uniform educational pattern to be pegged at the level of the average, and an educational pattern that produced averageness would tend gradually to debase even the levels of that averageness. Though he did not live to see the day, the thing that was to happen later to the academic quality of not a few major urban university systems which were forced by the racial-equality pressures of the sixties to go to open-admission policies would have been a prize exhibit to give credence to that fear.

The cornerstone of his educational philosophy was that education is the function of the family, not the state and not the church. The parochial system in which he became involved made that its basic assumption. Different from the Roman Catholic philosophy by which it is the institutional church which does the educating through its parochial schools, the Christian Reformed Church's parochial schools were specifically the function of families, by way of associations of such families. This emphasis on the family as, if not the basic unit of society then certainly a most crucial one, showed up in a number of ways. The family was the basic unit of the church and religion is the function of the family. That was the basis for his opposition to the granting of suffrage to women; voting was to be done by households, and that meant in effect by the heads of households, who then relatively uniformly happened to be males. Had my father lived long enough to witness the deteriorations in family solidarity following the second world war, I confidently suspect we would have seen an editorial or two accounting for that deterioration by pointing to the many ways and large degrees to which the family functioning was simply dissipated, as much by the unanalyzed wishes of the members of the family as at the initiatives of the state.

So here we have again a clear instance of his holding to a belief, in this case in the parochial school idea, which for my father had a different kind of inspiration than it did for most proponents of the parochial school. His point would be wholly missed if all we could see in the public versus parochial school controversies was a clash between two institutions or power centers. He was able to zero in on the far more crucial issue of the quality of education that would result from an education seen as a function of the state or as a function of the family. What was at stake was the freedom of education.

But the honeymoon with the parochial educational system did not last long. Again, so far as my father indicates or seemingly could know, the issue was his pacifism, and I have no way of confirming or disconfirming whether this indeed was the case. There may be a surprise item or two in the background of this.

The Christian Reformed Churches, which were by far the dominant proponents of parochial education, were made up of a relatively more conservative constituency. This was not what we now know as typical Bible-belt conservatism, though the difference may be subtle. As compared even with the also conservative Reformed churches, they kept alive a much more powerful ethnic sense. They prided themselves especially on being "*the* covenant people." They also over the years kept alive their family and cultural ties with the Netherlands. The use of the Dutch language among them long outlasted its use among the Reformed Churches. And it is not surprising that they would, as a significant part of their ideological package, have a much more alive sense of Dutch nationalism.

If there is any surprise in this connection, it is that their spirit of Dutch nationalism was not set over against a sense of American nationalism. While holding on to the first they also managed the neat trick of being perhaps as strongly pro-American as any group in this country. And this is where we get back to the connection with the pacifist issue. Their pro-America stance expressed itself in a keen and vocal patriotic ardor, and like all patriotisms, this was intensified in war-time. One of its most respected ideological spokesmen simply equated pacificism with treason, to general nods of approval from the lay and clerical constituency. "Pacifism" and "Liberalism" were equally dirty words.

Nor is this the whole of the story. The Christian Reformed Church constituency historically has been one of those rare minority groups which was able to do two things at once: to hold vigorously to its ideals of group purity and integrity, and at the same time within the group structure to labor effectively to outdo its "world" at its own games—to build not only its own schools but to produce a better education, to develop its own businesses but to be better businessmen. And America surely owes a debt of gratitude to those who successfully turn this rare trick. And, back to the point now at issue, that constituency seemed to have included a strong impulse not only to be patriotic like other patriots but to be more patriotic—not only in the sense of being noisier ones but in the more important sense of moving by the force of its patriotism to perpetuate America's more ideal traditional values.

And there was another factor involved, though it is impossible to assess exactly how strong a role it played. The story of the intense anti-German feelings that swept the country during and after the first World War is a familiar one. And the Dutch people were left quite uncomfortable by that. They, too, were from the same general area of Europe as the Germans were, and they could never be sure that in the popular mind they were not being confused with Germans. The adjective "Deutsch," applied to the Germans, was uncomfortably like the adjective "Dutch" applied to the Netherlanders. It is not surprising therefore, given some fear that in the popular mind they were indistinguishable from the Germans, that the Dutch would, in self-defense, take steps to widen the difference between themselves and the Germans by, among other things, raising the pitch of their patriotic fervor.

All of this, by the only evidence I have, which is my father's word, is the context in which his tenure in the parochial system became not only uncomfortable but untenable. I have no idea of what mechanics might have been employed to sever the connection but it was clearly not by his own resignation. This severance had to be a particularly painful one, among other reasons because it was a severance from a niche which he found to be so congenial to his own deep commitments on education. It was a hard-to-bear rejection "by his own." And this time the steady run of fortuitousness which had seen to it that when he was out of one thing another was there to step into failed him. Now, as at other times later, he was left simply to create his own thing. The chronology is a little uncertain as to whether it was for a period of one year or two, but the the next year or two he devoted himself, to use his own certainly euphemistic phrase, to "private teaching."

I am puzzled by the fact that there is mention of an income of five hundred dollars a year from that private teaching. That would certainly indicate that the private teaching was not confined to his teaching his own children at home. We at least were in no position to pay him a salary for that. But though I was one of the children he did teach at home, I have no recollection of there being anyone else's children involved. I have to venture the long guess that there could have been some adult teaching involved, but I am very unsure of that. What is certain is that he did for that next year (or two) keep his children at home and put them through a regular (and rigorous!) program of daily instruction.

There is more than a little pathos involved in that scene, which even the fact of my father's excellent teaching competence can scarcely temper. If the image of having to scrape along on a mere five hundred dollars a year is there, that has to be softened considerably by the fact that he did have his sixteen acre farm which by his own efforts and ingenuities did make him relatively self-sufficient economically. Much less than the typical family's budget outlays would suffice. The pathos is much more to be associated with the fact that he did have his back to the wall professionally, that he did strive so manfully to manage his circumstances, but most of all that he had to fight so hard to preserve his own self-respect by finding some great principle that he could turn the circumstances into.

But that "matter of principle" was not hard to come by. It was involved in the issue of parental rights versus the state's rights vis-a-vis children, an issue which has never been put wholly to rest, as evidenced by the periodic recurrence of it in specific cases, mostly involving the right of parents to educate their own children. And it did reach a climactic moment which proved not a little frightening to all of us. I have vivid recollections of the county sheriff and his deputy arriving at the door one evening. All the children were sent off to their bedrooms upstairs, but in those days every house was fitted with openable air "registers" in the floors between the lower and upper floors. This allowed for some heating of the bedrooms. That evening we did some pushing and shoving to determine whose ear might be pressed to the grille to hear what might be going on in the living room below. A loud argument ensued, which ended with my father's being hauled off to spend the night lodged in the town jail. When reading later of the terrible "knock at the door at night" which was to become the frightening and all-too-real focal sound of human repression, I had at least something in my own experience to connect it with.

How the issue was resolved I have no recollection. I do know that my father was released the next day and the home lessons went on as if nothing had happened, and for the balance of the school year. What would have happened had the summer not brought a new job opportunity I have no way of guessing. In retrospect, and whatever merits there might be in theory in the assertion of parental rights over the state's rights to education to one side, it was extremely fortunate that the private education episode was of as short a duration as it was. Had it gone on longer it would surely have generated in all of us a spirit of estrangement from the world around us, something we were already somewhat close to in view of my father's general spirit of estrangement from that world. It was a matter of some pride on his part to feel himself to be a person apart. While it was possible to discipline that feeling into channels of critical examination of that world's directions, for immature children to live in that kind of climate can be most damaging indeed.

The new job opportunity that offered itself meant a return to Harrison and the work of the Academy. This did involve a move from the homestead in Platte to which we had all become so deeply attached to a new home, which was to be ours for the next five years, in Harrison. But before carrying on that story I must turn back to pick up something else which was a major part of my father's life. This I have neglected so far simply because it deserves a chapter of its own.

VII
Marriage and the Family

I have mentioned my father's teaching of his own children at home, and I had better hurry now to legitimate those children by giving some account of how they got there. There were by then seven of us, minus one who had died in infancy, with another on the way (and two more to come after that before the family would be complete). Yes, there had been a marriage.

And it is hard to find adequate images to describe it. "Fairy-tale marriage" comes to mind. So does "marriage made in heaven." It had to be that; nothing short of heaven could have contrived so genuine a marriage beginning with so improbable a pair. And for good measure we need to throw in an only slightly altered version of the Pygmalion/My Fair Lady plot.

The "fairy-tale romance" image would need a little refurbishing to fit. One does have to replace, at least from where my mother's family must have seen it, the classic image of the tall, dark, and handsome young prince dashing in on his white charger to rescue the meek little maid from some unhappy plight, then to ride off to live happily ever after. In his place put a short-statured preacher from away out in nowhere, of uncertain livelihood, easily old enough to have been the father of their youngest daughter and the fourteenth of their fifteen children, special because she was still at home when the older children had married and gone on to lives of their own. That this dubious image could well have been going on in their minds I must infer from the fact that the marriage sounds something like an elopement even though without the proverbial ladder to the second-floor window and without the proverbial shotgun pursuit. That is reinforced by the fact that except for the years after my father died my mother lived in a nearly complete and, except for a moment here and there, painful estrangement from her family.

The image of the little broken-down preacher does need some correction. A studio portrait of my father from those days really was quite impressive, with nothing in the background of the picture to betray his short stature, his later Ben-Gurion style hair all neatly in place, his beard and moustache neatly clipped, his "preacher's suit" complete with vest and cutaway coat showing off to good effect the erectness of his posture, one hand thrust, Napoleon-like, into his vest, the other holding his later trade-mark black derby, his eyes bright with his visions—with all of this he really did not look to be that bad a bargain for a little girl from the farm. Even the everlasting necktie which through most of his years was to be his nemesis as far as tying it was concerned (but without which he would not venture out even to hoe the garden) was neatly tied and in place. The picture had its later interest not because it looked like him but because it did not, as his appearance seemed gradually to matter less and less to him. But he had a nice retort to efforts by my mother to hold the line: he simply pointed out how much he had in common with Charlie Chaplin—the shortness of stature, the black derby, the not exactly tidy clothes, and, though he was not in his own mind a comic figure, he could boast and justly that he had a natural flair for recognizing and chuckling over the comic.

Whether the romantic had been, over the years, a part of either his instinct or experience it is hard to say. The rather prevailing image he gives is of one extremely shy even to the point of bumbling embarrassment in the presence of women, and having to be rigorously self-disciplined in his relations to them since a bachelor preacher was *per se* held in suspicion, so that he had to be scrupulously alert against even the slightest gestures toward him from mothers who had probably spinster daughters to marry off. The intimations in the late-in-life autobiographical novel that he wrote, of at least suppressed romantic impulses are probably but not provably embellished for literary effect. There is one extant poem from those days expressing in exquisite and beautiful good taste his very genuine sadness at the breaking up of a relation that seemed to have held some promise.

But as compared to whatever else there might have been, the girl who became our mother was clearly "it." Their paths had first crossed (they were married at the start of 1909) seven years earlier. In the year of my father's graduation from Seminary, because he had plans to go on to graduate school, he agreed to serve a summer term in that parish out in New Sharon in south central Iowa, a summer term which grew into a term of two summers and a year. During that period he lived in the home of Anton and Eva Schippers, farmers, several of whose fifteen children were grown, obviously leaving some room in what had to have been a sizable house. Among those still at home was twelve year old Nellie, apparently an outgoing and playful little girl who, as the account indicates, dangled now and then on the Dominie's knee. Somewhere along the way, whether playfully and casually is not known but probably it was, my father declared that when she grew up he would come back and marry her. At least in the presence of this twelve year old, he was not too shy to declare his proposal. Just how seriously my mother-to-be took this is not very clear either, but after he had left New Sharon and gone on first to his year at Yale and then on to South Dakota, she did carry on some correspondence with him, in the form of simply being the correspondent for the family, taking it upon herself to keep him posted on the family news. But to either one of them or both the purportedly family-news letters seem not to have been confined to just that significance, for we find my father making a trip to New Sharon somewhere during my mother's eighteenth year—not just a side trip to some other trip but a trip solely for the purpose of looking her up. It is hard to determine whether his or her initiatives were the greater. The autobiographical novel which he wrote in the forties opens with a chapter telling of that visit to New Sharon. It is hard to know how much of that is fact and how much fiction in that description, but it is a story beautifully and ardently told.

Later details are somewhat uncertain since there is, besides the description in the novel, also a daily financial ledger which was begun a week before the marriage date and it by itself leaves a slightly different impression of how things worked out. The differences in the two accounts are of no great importance, involving at best the issue of whose initiatives may have run a shade ahead of whose. In the fall of the year of the New Sharon visit we find my mother showing up in Platte, ostensibly to "visit friends," though it is very unclear how she might have gotten to know anyone in Platte other than my father, so we have to suspect that she was really out to see him. As the novel has it, however, she was the guest at many social affairs arranged by the young people and the object of many attentions from the town's swains. There is a very hilarious account of how one of the leading ladies of the parish put on a sizable social affair which included older people and younger; somewhere during the evening, the older people gravitated to one part of the house and the younger to another. My father, as, after all, the minister, was trapped into the society of the older folk, while my mother naturally gravitated toward the people of her own age. So he (and maybe she) spent the evening eating his heart out having to listen to the gaieties that emanated from the next room. But as the party broke up, he simply walked in and announced that he was seeing her home. Things moved very rapidly and within weeks we find him announcing to his parish on a Sunday that he was taking off a couple of days during the week to be married. It is not wholly clear whether the announcement came during the time of my mother's visit to her "friends" in South Dakota, or whether she had gone back to her home in New Sharon. But early one morning in January they were wed in the Old First Church of Sioux Center, and after a pancake breakfast they took off, via special livery (!)—surely the only time in his life that my father indulged in that luxury—for the railroad station fifteen miles away where they could catch a train for South Dakota. And so they did live happily ever after.

It is hard to overdo the account of how closely interwoven those two lives became. The difference in ages—she was eighteen and he thirty-eight—simply proved to be no barrier. Nor did the difference in education. My mother's formal education had ceased at the end of the sixth grade, and presumably she had at that time dropped out of school to go to work. My father on the contrary was a college, seminary, and university graduate whose obsessions had been with the academic life. Apparently just after they were married a process of education for my mother began, but surely not at all as if to erase what might have been an embarrassing gap between them as far as education was concerned. My father simply was the inevitable teacher, and my mother simply the interested and eager student endowed with an extraordinary degree of natural intelligence not only for the conduct of daily affairs but for the quiet mastery of the formal academic disciplines. She eagerly absorbed under my father's tutelage the mysteries of literature, of Latin, of algebra and the like. This was, of course, the Pygmalion-theme in their lives, with the important difference that where Pygmalion loved his creation only after it was done, my father loved his from the beginning.

It is correct to say of my father and mother that they were simply, completely and unambiguously devoted to each other, and without interruption or a decline into routineness. My mother completely identified her life with his, and sought no meaning for her life apart from its meaning for his. And this happened not out of duress, nor even, I think, because of the then current social sense that a woman upon marriage was assumed to become an appendage of her husband's life, nor in the sense that he, by the sheer forcefulness of his own personality overwhelmed hers. My mother identified with him simply because she loved him completely, as he did her. She developed her own native talents, which were not inconsiderable. Her outlets, given the times and the circumstances, were few, but she developed a healthy poetic competence of her own, which found its expression in her freedom in writing poems for all manner of special occasions, such as birthdays and anniversaries. She became an able teacher, finding her outlet there in teaching in the church school, for which she was much in demand without interruption in her lifetime until in her later years her health failed. She became heavily involved in temperance work through the

Women's Christian Temperance Union. And when, as the crown of her life, she was named the Mother of the Year for the state of Iowa in 1949, that was also a crown for my father's life, and he was honestly happy then to bask in her glory without claiming any of the credit for her life's accomplishments. I have no doubt at all that it was that event more than any other, more even than his re-appointment after the lapse of fifteen years and at the age of seventy-eight to the editorship of the newspaper for two years until it folded because its Dutch-speaking constituency had largely died off—it was this that enabled him to forget how much of a hard struggle his own life had been and to live his final five years in a spirit of mellowed contentment. Through all of their life together she was his constant confidant. And among the nostalgic sounds that still linger indelibly in our recollections are the sounds of the clatter of the old kitchen range as at five o'clock *every* morning, my father began the day by kindling a fire, followed soon by the smell of the coffee-pot, and after that the drone of their voices as for an hour at the start of the day they had their time together. My mother did not really have or crave a life of her own, in the sense that she made my father's interests hers, and my father had no life of his own, in the sense that he had no interests or thoughts he could not wholly share with her.

The care and effort which he lavished on the homestead to which he brought his young bride can well stand as a symbol of his deep affection for her. Out of almost nothing but foresight and ingenuity and much hard work they built a place to live that was really quite idyllic. Besides the land he had managed to buy earlier there was not much to start with. The tiny church building in which the Platte parish had been housed had been outgrown, and when plans were initiated to build a larger structure, he purchased the old building. And by the time I came along it had been remodelled into a very substantial, ample, and well-planned dwelling which included the luxury of a solarium where my mother could indulge her love of flowers.

But perhaps even more special than the well-appointed house were the trees, all of them of my father's planting. In a countryside where no trees grew naturally, he managed to raise up to twenty-seven different varieties. Their arrangement which divided the sixteen acres into subplots each with its appropriate use in the larger scheme of things was simply idyllic. He spoke of the planting of trees as "almost like an article in my religious creed". "When a man plants a tree," he wrote, "he plans to stay; with the rooting of the tree the planter plants himself." The family mythology, which may be wholly or at least in part correct on this point, has it that virtually all the trees in that fairly well-wooded town were there by his hand, most of them American elms of which he had become so enamoured during his year in the "elm city" of New Haven.

The home and its setting together spoke really quite eloquently of my father's love for decent and dignified possessions, despite the steady note of abstemiousness that runs through his account of his earlier years and again later. He was no spiritist, disdaining delight in at least that much physical possession. Nor was he an ascetic by nature, nor a stoic; if there was stoicism at all, it was as a last resort, when the effort at material achievement proved futile, and not as a first resort, which would make the attainment of decent comfort irrelevant.

This bespeaks a wholesome interest in and appreciation for things, for living well, even though at their most expansive his tastes would be quite modest. And we did eat well, especially as far as wholesome food was concerned. Decent clothing was a little more problematic, but in a community such as Platte exchange of outgrown clothing among families was a commonplace. All in all, the life on the Platte homestead was quite delightful. There was so much to do and love and take delight in. It was a world of growing things, a world of cats and pigs and chickens and cows and calves and horses—everything to delight a growing boy's heart, the stuff of which nostalgia is made.

But that is only one part, and perhaps not even the dominant part, of my father's very complex disposition toward things. Nor is this matter of his relation to things at all a trivial aspect of his life. I think it played a major role, not only in the sense that what he called his version of Darwin's "struggle for existence" preempted so much of his time and energy. More influential even than that was the fact that the complexity of his attitude toward things led him, more than anything else did, into some eccentricities which had an inhibiting effect on his influence, as well as having a somewhat negative effect on his relation to his children. It is a matter of record, I suppose, that the religiously and ethically intense have peculiar difficulties in coming to terms with things. (Or is it the non-intense who have the difficulties?)

Actually, there was no explicit "philosophy of things" in his repertoire. His disposition toward things was quite completely simply the corollary of two more nearly overt commitments. It was in part a corollary of his sense of Christian calling to be "a servant." This involved not wholly an act of will, since this was so congenial to his native temperament. It was the reverse side of the coin of his natural self-effacement. And the ambiguity that is, not uncommonly, associated with that is that exactly those whose sense of calling is the most intense are the ones most certain to live in a kind of haunting fear that they are not taking their calling seriously enough. In that kind of context my father lived apparently by a sense that even in the enjoyment of a modicum of physical comforts the purity of that calling might be compromised. The other drive that coloured his disposition toward things was his relation to other persons, notably the fear of being a burden to them or expecting more from them than he had a right to ask. This is clearly exemplified in some of our later experiences. Down the road a few years when some of us were in our early teens we did become entrepreneurs enough to hire ourselves out to plow gardens in the spring. Whenever such an opportunity came along, we were given exact directions as to how much we should charge the customer, which, believe me, was never very much. We soon got wise to the trick of not stating to our clients what our charges were, in effect not charging anything (for which my father could not have faulted us, in a way). But what we were really doing was letting the customer offer what seemed to him a just wage. We easily made on the average double what the asking price might have been—and for good measure we developed a fair amount of dramatic talent as we reenacted for my father's benefit the scenario of how the customer had pleaded with us to accept what he said was his wholly unworthy offer.

In retrospect it is a good deal easier than at the time to see how on this score one laudable virtue had become twisted into something very different. His admirable glorying in his self-reliance in dealing with the sometimes hard natural circumstances of his life sometimes quite obviously degenerated into a glorying in the fact that life was hard. But matters did not stop even there. The glorying in hardship became itself, though not by design, a process of making circumstances harder than they needed to be. The aggressive fight against hardship, oddly, ends up being an aggressive pursuit of hardship—"aggressive poverty" would be an apt phrase to use. Something obviously had gone awry with the spirit of Calvinistic austerity by the time it had caught up with my father. If we can believe Weber's classic thesis in *Protestantism and the Rise of Capitalism*, that austerity had compelled ordinary mortals into an aggressive quest for material success. Not so my father.

Nor is this an idle guess. That spirit of aggressive poverty, of a near-flaunting of one's hardships, became explicit and overt in his proud boast that never once in his life did he drive a car (though an item in the family mythology says that he did, once, only to end up, by the most direct possible route, in a ditch). He seemed quite oblivious to the fact that because he did not drive a car, many others were put to some effort to facilitate his getting where he had to be. Or the aggressive poverty image is explicit in the fact that during one of those periods between employments when he simply had no visible means of supporting himself and his family, he did receive an invitation to become the minister of a reasonably substantial parish in Iowa—an invitation which immediately found its way into the wastebasket without any acknowledgement of its having been received ever being sent.

For that matter, this near-flaunting of poverty was more immediately embodied, and at some cost to such pride as a seven-year-old can be expected to have mustered, in the event which can properly be titled his discovery of the corn cob. Certainly his struggle for survival was over the years as much a struggle to keep warm as a struggle to be fed, and all kinds of ingenuities were resorted to as defense against the howling prairie winter winds beating on loosely constructed homes, long before insulation had been invented. In the context of this struggle he discovered the corn cob, which to a farmer tends to fall into the same class as eggshells and banana peels as paragons of uselessness. But corn cobs do burn, fast and furiously, which is the problem. It became a near full-time job on cold days to be stoking the fires. But these were corn-cobs with a difference and surely only my father would have thought of it. One of the great things about Platte was that it not only had a railroad but it was the end of the railroad line. And one of the truly nostalgic recollections of Platte was the experience of walking the two or three blocks to the railroad station in the morning to see the daily train take off, and back at seven at night to see it come in. As my father's imagination was carried far beyond the dikes of Friesland by watching the ships sailing out and in on the canals, mine was carried by a little passenger train. But where there is a railhead there is also a facility for holding livestock preparatory to its being shipped off to, in this case, the Sioux City markets. And there were also pens for holding the livestock for a few days before shipment; but that also meant that there was bound to be corn for feeding them—and cobs, a *lot* of cobs. But these cobs had been trampled well into the eight or ten inches of goo which only a herd of swine or beef cattle confined to a tiny feedlot could produce, and if the cobs were to be had they must obviously be rescued from the goo. So out they came, basket after basketfull, to be carted home—an utterly forbidding and humiliating menial task. But once allowed to dry, they ended up well-caked with dried pig dung, and, incredibly to any who are familiar with the impossible stenches associated with a pig-pen, they were also quite odorless. Best of all, they burned, and they burned, and they burned—indeed, they had to be the greatest fuel invention since the "buffalo chips" which kept many a pioneer from freezing to death. But, I remember beginning to ask even then, only to myself, "Why do we always have to be doing things the hard way?"

This dismal experience was, however, and emphatically, the exception in what then and in nostalgic recollection loomed as a pleasant, even care-free, and idyllic life for my father and his growing family. The twenty mile move to Harrison in 1923 where my father was to teach for the next five years in the Academy did not change this image. The family life continued in much the same mood, though, if anything, in an even more carefree environment. We lived within a block of the Academy, so that the days of my father's extended absences from home could be cheerfully forgotten. The same hardships had to be faced and the same uncertainties about whether or not the gardens and fields would be productive, but at least he was more constantly on the scene than he had ever been before. Harrison was a wide-open town for children. We could roam freely its full half-mile length and breadth and ride our horses anywhere we pleased, unhampered by anyone's fences or other evidences of boundary lines.

It was during those years much more than any others that I experienced a closeness to my father. This was highlighted by, again, the struggle to keep warm and what efforts had to go into managing that. This time that struggle involved travelling back to Platte with team and wagon, this time to transport firewood—surely a step upward from the stockyard and its cobs. A good part of the "woods" that my father had coaxed into growing on our Platte homestead had fallen victim to an exceptionally hot and dry summer—or to some infestation—and the now dead trees were available for our use. The round trip took some six or seven hours, including loading time, so that if we left in mid-afternoon after school was out for the day, it would be dark long before we arrived home. And I do mean dark; we carried no lights along the seldom-travelled route. Some of my own most unforgettable times with my father were those, riding along through the rather cold autumn nights, with the vast canopy of the stars, which was a special feature of Dakota because of its almost always clear atmosphere. Then the long hours were pretty well divided between my father's pointing out to me the mysteries of the recognizable constellations in the sky and his singing the old familiar hymns, as the horses plodded steadily homeward. It was also on such trips that he began telling me about Immanuel Kant and his famous "two things fill me with wonder and awe, the starry heavens above and the moral law within"—so that to this day I cannot look up at the former without being reminded of the latter. Then, too, I think for the only times in his life, he would sometimes apologize for having failed to make life easier than it was for his family. Or he spoke of his hopes and fears for the world—all to a twelve-year-old boy. And when the hymns did get on to being about a heavenly father, I remember wondering, in childish innocence or heterodoxy, why people made so much ado about a father far off in the sky when I had a father so close by my side.

The Harrison years were the relatively patterned years. There was plenty of hard work for each, but this was simply accepted as a habit, with no clear awareness of it being so many daily duties overtly imposed. It was as though everything could move along indefinitely on this even keel. The future and whatever demands it might bring seemed very far away.

Other than revolving about the daily work routines, the family life centered about mealtimes which were so much more than just mealtimes. For one thing it was simply assumed that everyone would be there for mealtimes and three times a day. But accompanying the mealtimes were my father's version of family devotions, which he turned into a major educational process in itself. There were the prayers, of course, which often turned into a general indirect commentary, presumably for the benefit of the divine, on the events of the day. There were readings, which might be from the family Bible, but they might also take the form of readings, serial-fashion, from significant books which had made their way into the household, often by borrowing from friends. It might be something about Tolstoi, or a biography of John Wesley (which left an early predilection for ecumenism), or Abraham Muste on pacifism. If the reading was from the Bible, it might be in English or Dutch, or even in Greek or in Hebrew. My father had for most of his life made a great deal of the art of memorization. Even in his first stint at the Academy he would memorize the history lesson and possibly more. (There was a rumor, which he later disavowed, that he had memorized a whole book of propositions in geometry in a couple of hours.) On his preaching engagements he made it a regular habit to recite the day's biblical lesson from memory, and at the time of the observance of the sacraments he was in the habit of repeating the lengthy accompanying liturgy from memory. Memorization did not have the bad connotations it has for most of us, as expressed in our references to "mere memory," or "mere rote learning." That bad image that memorization had acquired had to rest on a mistaken image of the memorization process, as if it could happen simply by frequency of repetition. For my father memorization called for the most intense attention to the substance of the material—he learned by grasping the flow of ideas rather than relying on the consecution of sounds. In his later years the memorization discipline took on the added dimension of being a deliberate effort to resist the deteriorations of the mental faculties. But back in those earlier years, the family gathered around the table became the audience for the recitations of what had been memorized that day. And at least the breakfast prayers often consisted in a recitation of the Lord's Prayer in some foreign language. Oddly, whenever he decided to do the Lord's Prayer in German, he would introduce it by announcing, "today we pray with the Kaiser"—oddly, because the Kaiser, of all people, stood for the kinds of things my father had found least congenial to his own commitments.

This image, of my father engaging in a many-sided educational process while carrying out his role as the veritable "autocrat of the breakfast table," is also useful in saying something quite exact about the nature of our family life. That process had to be a broadening educational experience, to be sure. But it also meant that the family's role was mainly that of being an audience, and pretty much a captive one. This posture, I must now say in long retrospect, left a pervasive and quite inarticulate undercurrent of feeling, despite what must have been his best will to the contrary, that we were not so much participants as recipients and observers. And in consequence of that, whatever ties might have bound one family member to another, these were overshadowed by the larger fact that what we had in common with each other was really that we had together been the common spectators, and in a wholly non-pejorative sense, of my father's "performance." It surely would be an ungracious slander to suggest that he did not hold each of us, and equally, in a powerful affection. No personal sacrifice was held to be too great for our well-being, and particularly to assure a higher education for us all. But the warmth of mutuality between him and us was somewhat lacking—though by the standards of the family-ethos of that time and place that was not too unusual. Individuality was neither overtly fostered nor interfered with. But it is clear, again only in long retrospect, that what was happening was that each of us, unpremeditatedly and inwardly, was defining himself or herself by our attitudes and relations to his dominating presence. And each came out, I think, quite differently.

The simple life in the simple village of Harrison did come to an end, but this time not as other professional assignments had come to an end, somewhat mysteriously and for no clear reason, only to find some fortuitous new possibility coming along to provide him with an outlet and a means of livelihood. This change did come about by clear design and as a result of a more aggressive job-seeking than had taken place on any other occasion of transition. The urge for change came from the fact that the older children were now getting along through their high school years, and as strong as any ambition he had ever had there was his ambition that his children would have the benefits of a college education. The oldest, a sister, had gotten off to college, but there were eight more in the educational pipeline, and it was clear that with his meager resources there would be no way in which he could fulfill that ambition for a college education for all.

If there was a fortuitous circumstance involved then, it was that in 1928, the Academy in Orange City, which he had always held in the highest esteem, became the jumping off place for the beginning of a Junior College. This was but one such venture in the state of Iowa, which was in the process of developing a very extensive program of Junior Colleges. A move to Iowa would not only put the first two years of college within reach but would contain the added bonus of making it possible for those still in high school to reap the benefits of the Academy's excellent education. So obviously appealing was all this that for once a new position, now in Orange City, became a must—enough so as to overcome his habitual reticence in seeking a position.

The most obvious possibility to look into was that of a position on the faculty of the new Junior College. And again, there are some unresolved puzzles connected with his application for a position there. His credentials by that time had to be good enough to warrant serious consideration. And obviously he was given such consideration, enough so to lead him to believe when we all went to Iowa in August for his mother's burial that he had such a position in hand. The mystery involves why, apparently after having received some kind of assurances, that possibility fell through.

But something else did materialize. A weekly Dutch-language newspaper, *De Volksvriend*, was being published in Orange City, and it was a substantial and well-established private enterprise. He did secure an appointment as its editor. I have no way of knowing whether, in taking that position, he was able to do so with full enthusiasm or whether those years were marked by a feeling that his first love really had been and still was teaching. As it turned out, and wholly by my judgment, the editorship did offer him a better chance to do what he was especially qualified for than even a college teaching position would have been. For though as editor he did have to perform each week some dull routine editing chores, he was a natural writer. Furthermore, he had always had and over the years strongly developed a lively interest in pretty nearly everything that was going on in the life of the community and of the larger world. For him every event invited reflection and critical appraisal. The next six years were, I judge, among his most productive years intellectually. They surely burnished his image as an exceptionally intelligent and far-seeing person. And I have no reason to doubt that, though his hope for a teaching position had been disappointed, he could throw himself into this new and quite undreamed of position with spontaneous enthusiasm.

VIII

Pacifism

My father was a pacifist. There surely are no doubts about that. But this feature of his intellectual and moral-instinctual make-up was also one of his most complex features. Everything that one wants to say about this to make it simple becomes problematic as soon as it is said.

We can start with the question, for example, of how large this loomed in his thinking and in his career. As far as his image in the eyes of others is concerned, it probably loomed pretty large. Few people who knew him would have failed to think "pacifist" whenever they thought of him. But even here it is not wholly clear whether what was uppermost in that image was its substance or its mode. I rather judge that for the most part it was somewhat less the fact that it was a commitment to pacifism that struck people than that it was a commitment of a certain kind, not so much *that* he was a pacifist as *how* he was a pacifist. And whatever singularity there was about him in the public image, and whatever favorable judgment that public image was to contain, had more to do with the intensity of the commitment than what it was a commitment to.

But how large did the particular pacifist image loom in his own self-image? It is clear that there was on his part some chagrin at his simply being equated with pacifism. There is an extant poem which, though not exactly to this point, says something that has a bearing on it. It is an expression of dismay at the manner in which we go about simply labelling people, supposing that once we have them labelled we can be done with them. Once we know what they are, we suppose, we no longer need to deal with them. Once we can call a man a pacifist, we no longer need to deal with the issue which the pacifist raises. In an allied sense, I think my father had some feeling that his image as a pacifist simply obscured, in the minds of some, any other talent or interests he might have had. This is linked with his supposition, of which I shall have more to say, that his being a pacifist on numerous occasions barred him from certain desired professional opportunities.

If that much suggests that the importance of his pacifism was overrated in relation to all his other interests, then other evidence suggests the contrary, that pacifism was a main passion of his life. This evidence consists mainly in the fact that he seemed constantly to be raising the pacifist issue in his writings and that he did this for a very long time—at least from before the first World War until long after the second. The relative frequency of his comments on war surely suggests that he identified with pacifism more than with any other issue. That impression is reinforced by a touching gesture at the end. At his request concerning his funeral, which he planned himself down to the minutest detail, he was buried with a copy of his little book, *Ten Eeuwigen Vrede* (Towards Eternal Peace) lying over his heart. The book had gotten its title from Immanuel Kant's small work on the same topic. True, the title under those special conditions may have spoken more explicitly of his anticipation of the peace of his eternal rest than of a world freed from the curse of war. But who can fault a man for, at the end, blending all his utlimate goals together under the enticing and all-comprehending image of "Peace"?

One searches I think in vain for any answer to the question why my father ever became a pacifist. After all, not many people are avowed pacifists, and when some are, one wonders why they are while others are not. There was nothing in his cultural environment or heritage, as a child or later, that could be plausibly invoked to account for it. The Dutch were, after all, quite unabashed imperialists, and they gloried as much as any imperialists in their historic military exploits by which they had first wrenched themselves loose to become a national identity and then carved out for themselves a world-wide empire. And the Dutch who came to the middle west of America were mainly political conservatives for whom the mantenance of national power, if need be by force of arms, was an automatic high priority. To find in the Reformed churches persons who had some sympathy for pacifism one had to look to New York, where even the Dutch Reformed had been touched by eastern liberalism's critical disposition towards war.

The only thing one can say in this connection is that my father became a pacifist from the inside. In this as in everything he thought about he was clearly a self-determined person. He did not learn his pacifism (or anything else) from anyone else. He was not an "aper," as he said, but aimed to be a "shaper." He read others and cited them, but quite strictly only in the sense that they were saying, perhaps in fresh idioms, what he already believed or knew. That holds not merely for his pacifism but for everything else. He walked through life not waiting to be influenced or shaped by life; rather he went about with his antennas alert to pick up what they were already attuned to. Nor did he rely on the sounds of other peacemakers to reinforce or strengthen his own peacemaking sensitivities. When he believed something he was predisposed to believe it, at least in this case, with a furious and unquestioning fervor.

When he encountered people who held other convictions than his own, this did not, in connection with pacifism or anything else, drive him back in upon himself to reexamine his own commitments. The only way he knew to respond to opposition was to intensify his commitments. This circumstance enormously complicated how we have to think about his pacifism, and left him in a somewhat different posture than, for instance, the more renowned pacifist, A. J. Muste. Serious as Muste was in his pacifism, he never lost his buoyancy, his optimism. If he is rememberable as "the happy warrior" for peace, my father must be remembered for the intense somberness of his pacifist stance. To him as a pacifist, his world was, in Luther's phrase, a world "with devils filled." And opposition to pacifism was not, to him, merely a difference of viewpoint, it was a personal affront.

But because of that circumstance, it is not always clear exactly what the issue was or who the enemy was. Ostensibly pacifists simply oppose the appeal to war as a way of dealing with the problems of the world. That obviously means that pacifists are opposed to the people who advocate or are responsible for the recourse to war. But in my father's case it may have been that the villains he had chiefly in mind were the ones who failed to espouse the pacifist radicalism, especially the clergy. If the specter of war was frightening enough for its own sake, the very idea of waging war acquired an extra demonic dimension simply by virtue of the fact that it was so hard to find converts to pacifism or even to find people who, though not pacifist themselves, would treat pacifism as a possible option to be considered. There is a sense in which it was hard to know who the real villains were, the military or the non-pacifist clergy who kept uttering their blessings on war.

But my father was never troubled by such complexities, if not in pacifism, then in the psychology of the pacifist. For him, as for the morally intense generally, the issue, whatever its correct identification might be, was simply reduced to black and white terms. The only two alternatives were peace and war. He was never able to identify with those who wrestled, not with the issue simply of peace or war, but of fighting or not fighting. If everything were simply reducible to terms of peace or war, the whole world might well be pacifist by instinct. What my father may well have failed to reckon with is that there may be circumstances in which the consequences of not fighting could be more deplorable even than the consequences of fighting. I mention this only to provide a context for understanding that for my father, everyone was simply against him in his pacifism, even those who saw in war, however terrifying its prospects and consequences were, an evil that was less than the evil that might follow should we simply fold our hands and acquiesce in the evil designs of a Hitler. To even consider the possibility that under certain conditions war might be the lesser of two evils he saw as an act of weakness, of temporizing with the evil of war.

All of this complexity is perhaps most clearly brought into focus by pointing out that war was for him, in the last analysis, *morally* wrong. We do a lot of bandying about in these days of the term "moral" or "immoral." And it is not always clear what we mean. My father suffered no such confusion. He knew exactly what it meant to call something "morally" wrong. That meant that it was absolutely and unconditionally wrong, so that no circumstances could ever make it right or even mitigate its evilness. And, finally, the supreme immorality, oddly, may not have been the immorality of war itself but the immorality of failing to see that war was simply immoral—that is, unconditionally and absolutely and totally wrong. And because so few could share that exact stance toward war, he did naturally feel that he stood quite alone in his pacifism with the whole world against him. I do not think it ever occured to him that no one really wants war, even though some would opt for war against accepting the consequences of not fighting in some circumstances.

This is what I had in mind when, above, I made a distinction between the *substance* of my father's commitment (that it was a commitment against war) and its *mode* (how the commitment was held). And his claim to fame, or at least his singularity, lies rather in the second of these than in the first. Or, in other words, more important to an understanding of him than the fact that he was a pacifist was the fact that he was a moralist, and in the exact sense I have here given to that term.

But moralism was not the only idiom he used to express his commitment. He was not insensitive to the fact that among his constituency "moralism" was not exactly an honorific term, since it laid emphasis on human actions or human initiatives toward virtue, while Calvinism laid its stress on human depravity and on the initiatives of the divine grace. So, not self-consciously but spontaneously, he could employ with equal facility the other idiom, of commitment to doing the will of God, or of being pacifist as his duty to God. And if to be a non-pacifist, or anything less than radically pacifist in one's disposition toward war was the ultimate immorality, that could as readily be expressed in theological terms: to be non-pacifist or only mildly pacifist was one's ultimate disobedience to God—or the ultimate contradiction of one's commitment to God.

But both idioms had exactly the same meaning. And whichever idiom he employed, the ethical or the theological one, he really never argued the war-peace issue. He simply, in either way, declared war to be evil. And as such and only as such, he was a pure example of a man of conscience.

But conscience did not have for him the conventional image, of that which is there to haunt us when we go astray. Conscience was not for him the Socratic *daemon* which simply said no whenever he was inclined to go astray. Conscience was for my father a much more positive voice—it was his certainty that certain things, now notably war, were simply unqualifiedly evil.

How uncompromising he was on the war issue is exemplified by two items. The first goes back to the first World War, in the Platte days. There he did come under fire for his pacifism, and so far as he knew, that pressure blocked his entrance into or continuation in certain vocational opportunities. That is, of course, one major direct way of hurting a person for his pacifist positions. But there was another and possibly even more explicit way in which he came under pressure. I am not sure how to interpret the episode or measure the pressure, since this is one of those things that is subject to different interpretations. One must remember that in a typical small town like Platte, the pro-war sentiments in war time tended to run pretty high. And especially in Platte, as I have noted, the Dutch were not clearly differentiated in the public mind from the Germans and so were readily suspected of being at least weak in their patriotism. In more urban areas a pacifist could pretty well hide in the crowd, but not so in the small town. In small towns the dissenter is an instantly marked person, particularly when this is a dissent from the general patriotism that becomes fervent in war-time. One could come up with sizable catalogs of ugly incidents which occurred in small towns in the effort to frighten the dissenters into line, most of them prompted by the easy assumption that anyone who would oppose or question the war-effort would be at least flirting with treason.

In my father's case, the pressure, however strong it may have been, came in the tangible form of a pressure to purchase war bonds. The particular incident which exemplified the radicalness with which he clung to his pacifism involved his being waited on in his own home one evening by what I suppose was some sort of "committee" from the town to urge or demand that he buy war bonds, at least as a symbolic gesture toward patriotism. Possibly the committee was self-appointed. I have no knowledge of the details of what might have transpired during what had to be a stormy session. The story of its climax was often told later.

My father's reply finally was that if those who were urging him to buy the bonds insisted, he would turn over to them his home and acreage and be out of the house at eight o'clock the next morning. I have to believe that he meant it, though at a distance it could easily be read as an act of calling their bluff, or as a way of getting rid of some pesky salesmen. After all, what could they say after that? I doubt very much that my father was thinking in a very calculating way at the time, inwardly remembering that landed property is not transferable simply by announcing that tomorrow morning one will walk off it and leave it behind. He had too much of a temper to be so calculating.

The story did for a little while later on acquire a dramatic character which it did not deserve—as if the fact of the matter was that my father was faced with loss of his homestead if he did not recant his pacifist convictions. Willing he might have been to do that, but this was hardly, in a calmer perspective, either an actual penalty or an actual threat.

A much more realistic instance of paying a stiff price for his pacifist convictions came later, during the second World War. Then his own sons were of military age and, in varying degrees of immediacy, subject to the military draft. It was a major crisis for my father when one of them declined to go along with the pacifist doctrine, which would involve going through the regular procedures for filing as a conscientious objector. This obviously put my father in the tough position of having to choose between his convictions about the total evil of war (and the immorality of participation) and his love for his own sons. But in the conflict between these he opted for the principle, not merely in an inwardly passive way, but overtly by refusing to communicate with the son in any way during the three years of his service in the navy. Trivial, you say? By no means. Nothing in his life, I suppose, was more painful to him (or in another sense to my brother) than that. But nothing shows more clearly how much my father was willing to pay for his pacifist commitments. But maybe "commitments" is no longer the correct word. "Commitments" are made by us and by so much can be broken or redirected. Pacifism was rather a conviction by which he felt himself totally bound.

The easy charge which was levied against my father, and against pacifists generally, obviously was that this was, if not tantamount to treason against the country then at least terribly unpatriotic. But my father was an intensely patriotic person. And his patriotism was surely honest, and not just a prudential show put on to ward off the suspicion that he was anti-patriotic just because he was so radically opposed to war. On national holidays he religiously flew the national flag—and the term "religiously" here does not have the loose conventional meaning of "solemn regularity." It had a near-sacramental quality about it. At least in the South Dakota years, the Fourth of July holiday loomed larger than Christmas. During his newspaper days, his editorials in late June made strong pitches for making more and more of the community celebration of the Fourth, even though there were already large and well-attended community celebrations. The tragic old poem, *The Man Without a Country*, the story of one who had renounced his citizenship and was doomed to roam the world with no homeland anywhere, was an oft-repeated poem in our home's devotions. Love of country was for my father quite unabashedly a part of loving God. The hymns *America* and *O Beautiful for Spacious Skies* were a major item in the family's hymn-singing around the dinner table. (*Onward, Christian Soldiers* was obviously suspect because it was never clear whether this might have a specifically and literally militaristic connotation.) There simply was no way in which my father's patriotism could be faulted, unless, as so many thought, patriotism should be equated with the slogan, "My country right or wrong." For him all of life, individual and institutional, was subject to critical appraisal. Everything, he saw, was ultimately legitimated only by its being moral, and as far as country was concerned, war was its ultimate form of immorality.

But if as a pacifist he was easily suspect of being at best unpatriotic and at worst a traitor, this was not the only or even most frequent overt attack on him, this time mostly by the churches. There were pacifists in the churches but during war time they tended to be closet-pacifists. But mostly the churches had no love for pacifists. Though some clergy suffered no embarrassment from simply identifying the will of God with the national interest and, as circumstances seemed to warrant it, with the successful prosecution of the war, others obviously had to choke a bit over that. Then they reverted to making a charge against pacifism which was more indigenous to the churches' own character: then pacifists were charged with heterodoxy. The defenders of the war-effort then made their appeals mainly to the Bible, and in that mainly to the Old Testament image of the Hebrews' God who waged and won their battles for them. But among Calvinists the even more telling charge of heresy against pacifism was something else. Pacifists, it was held, committed the final unpardonable sin of contravening the biblical insistence on the divine sovereignty. In some sense that doctrine was interpreted to mean that wars were indeed the will of God, and they who were not willing to acknowledge this were committing the sin of presumptuousness, in being against what God was clearly for. The evil of pacifism was compounded by the fact that pacifism relied on human action rather

Pacifism

than putting themselves into subjection to God. In that context "ethics" and "morality" were terms with a negative connotation, though this would be more readily maintained in the contexts of overt debate on the war-issue than in the practical conduct of life.

What all of this reinforced for my father was his anxieties about making the Bible the last court of appeal of the churches, as the churches were committed to doing. This to him was but one more evidence that the appeal to biblical authority was an easily manipulable appeal. By it one could quite ingeniously find sanction for just about whatever he wanted to justify. And in that context, the exact thrust of much of his effort with respect to the pacifist issue was devoted, not so much to finding biblical sanction for pacifism, nor even to refuting those who appealed to the Bible for support for war, but to the milder task of showing that pacifism was not at all inconsistent with biblical teaching or the Calvinistic theological traditions.

He placed his higher reliance, as a pacifist, though he did not use the term, on a kind of "higher law," of the kind that finds its early articulation in Greek tragedy, an appeal which is the main inspiration throughout history for the human drive to humaneness in culture. His label for that was more likely to be "the appeal to conscience." Conscience, in his view, though it may vary with different individuals and cultures, was relatively less manipulable to suit our interests than was the appeal to Scriptures, or to anything outside ourselves. And he had some evidence for this out of his own complex defenses of pacifism. In the heat of debate over the war issue among the clergy, some probably foolishly extravagant statements were made on both sides. He was sensitive to the fact, though he seems to have been gracious enough not to skewer the opposition with this, that the pro-war people often did and had to retract, after the war passions had cooled, much of what they had impulsively proclaimed during the war. At least relatively, a pacifist remained free from having to retract what *he* had said in the heat of the debate. By that kind of evidence, my father was satisfied that conscience, despite whatever troubles we may have with defining its kind of appeal, was a surer guide to moral stability even than the appeal to the Bible or established church orthodoxy.

Nor was he overly impressed with the argument against pacifism that "there always have been wars and there always will be." Such fatalism about war simply played no part in his thinking. But to the extent that he encountered it, he had two lines of response to it, the first relatively mild but the second extremely radical. The first consisted in his strong advocacy of pacifism as an activism. Though his own pacifist language often fell into the general idiom of being "*against* war," his finer instincts insisted rather on being "*for* peace." He took literally the exact etymological point of the word "pacifism"—the pacifist is a peace-*maker*. But at the same time he had his troubles with the word "pacifism," wholly on the basis that by a phonetic accident, it came out sounding much like the word "passivism." He was similarly troubled by the negative connotation of the popular label for pacifists, "conscientious *objectors*." He pleaded, therefore, for a switching of terminology, from "pacifism" or "pacifist" to "pacigerent", to give the pacifist a vigorously aggressive image to at least match the aggressiveness we sense in the use of the term "belligerent". Peace is something the pacifist *wages*, like other people *wage* war. This insistence on giving pacifism a more aggressive image does not mean merely that if we do hold it in an aggressive manner we can eradicate war; it has the profounder aim of erasing our fatalistic image which says we are helpless before the phenomenon of war and making war over into something we simply must do something about.

The second response to the supposed inevitability of war is even more radical and far-reaching because it poses a latent challenge to something very basic in our conventional thinking about morality or about our duty. By that conventional thinking, our notion of what can defensibly be identified as our duty is contingent on our notion of what it is within our power to do. A person can hardly be held morally responsible to do what lies outside his power to do. Obvious as that seems on the face of it, we cannot be all that sure about what may be the limitations on our capacities. It is not easy to fix the exact meanings of this. Partly because of that, the ready appeal to "I can't" becomes a delightfully convenient appeal whenever we wish to evade our duty. "We cannot be morally judged for not opposing war, because there is no way in which we can affect the incidence of war." To all of that my father had a ready response, and though that has many problems of its own, his did have the special merit of resulting in the maintenance of moral seriousness where the rival notion admits of moral escapism. For him, it is not capacity to do that determines what we ought to do, but the converse. It is duty that defines capacity. What we must do we can do. This is, obviously, not meant to be a fact-statement nor is it defensible as such. It is a statement that comes naturally to a moralist, in the sense in which my father was a moralist. It is meant to deprive the would-be moralist of his most tempting escape from his moral obligation, the escape by the appeal to the impossibility of doing something. And pragmatically, it is a precondition for something like pacifism; hope of eradicating the specter of war must begin in the belief that it can be eradicated. It is also a major statement about the nature of man. He simply is not the victim of circumstances nor of his history: the fact that there always have been wars simply does not mean that there always have to be wars.

Though it was of the essence of the issue for my father to see that war is *morally* evil, in the sense that it must be seen to be unconditionally so (any exception to this is to temporize with the issue and fatally weaken one's stance against it), it was not that he did not articulate his reasons for opposing war. In fact, he was familiar with and gave expression to just about every argument against war that was known to man. The most telling of these was, properly, the enormous and direct and perceptible damage this did to persons who were involved, not only the physical destruction and the maiming of bodies but the psychological and spiritual damage to people, whether they were on the winning or the losing side. It was quite incredible to him that this side of war could be apparently so glibly brushed aside by the non-pacifists. Human life was not to him the kind of thing one treated calculatingly, as if it were the kind of currency one could be willing to put up in exchange for the benefits of winning. The content of his categorical moral imperative against war was the sanctity of human life. And though in the main he had only a word of condemnation for any who in any way participated in war, his instinct for people did not prevent him from ministering in whatever way he could to the broken men who returned from war.

When one gets past citing this frightful cost in people, as an argument against war, it is quite a different situation, which involves a basic inconsistency which my father was never aware of. It is the inconsistency between, on the one hand, taking the rigorous moral stance against war that he took, and on the other providing reasons for the stance. In the first case one is simply unconditionally opposed to war, and then no reasons are relevant; one in effect takes the absolutist stand and announces it rather than arguing for it. When, however, one presents arguments against war, each argument becomes simply a statement of a condition under which war is wrong. If, as he did in arguing for his pacifism, one cites the enormous economic costs of war, then war becomes legitimate by our willingness to pay the economic costs. Or if, as he also did, one argues that war in Europe is bad because it might lead to bombs falling on our own country, then war is approvable on the condition that we can keep the bombs from falling on us. Or if, as he also argued, militarism *per se* is bad because the mere possession of the capacity to make the appeal to military solutions will enhance the likelihood that we will, then militarism is only conditionally evil; it is evil only in the event that we do resort to force. In the context of "arguments" or "giving reasons" against war, one is no longer speaking the language of moral imperatives but the calculating pragmatic language of the marketplace.

An analogous situation must make this clearer and more concrete. Along with his rigorous moral stance against war my father was also, in a way as rigorously, opposed to the use of alcohol and tobacco. He was also against a lot of other kinds of things, but war, drinking, and smoking were in a class by themselves. The arguments against smoking were pretty much confined to economic reasons. The health issue involved was to rise to prominence only much later. Smoking was wrong simply because it cost too much, along with, of course, its being clearly an economic waste. That argument did once back-fire on my father. According to the story, which has all the earmarks of being the story of an actual occurrence, and interestingly could have come to be known only by his telling of it, he was once walking along a street in Sioux City. (That it was Sioux City adds to the interest of the story: to act as the guardian of the morals of his own Calvinistic town of Orange City was one thing, but to carry the crusade to the streets of a thoroughly "worldly" metropolis-like Sioux City was something else.) Along the way he spotted a man leaning against an apartment building smoking a cigar—of course, a "big, black cigar". He went up to him and began to chide him for wasting his money on smoking cigars. "Why," my father said, "if you now had all the money you have spent in your lifetime on cigars, you might well be able to own this apartment building." To which the man replied, "I do." This is certainly the classic case from my father's archives of the risk of giving specific reasons for not doing something. The specific reasons become the conditions that make something wrong. And when the conditions are not present, what otherwise is judged to be wrong becomes right. But, as I have pointed out, my father seems not to have been aware of the dilemma one faces who must insist, as he did with respect to war, that it is morally (unconditionally) wrong and at the same time spell out the reasons that make it wrong.

Of the three major items that stood at the center of his moral reform impulses, war, smoking, and drinking, it was his pacifist stance that he was able to defend most adamantly and without a waver. Next to that was the issue of drinking, but even there a circumstance developed late in life that led to his cracking just a bit on that. Sometime before his death he did suffer a heart attack, and his personal physician and long-time friend, old Doctor De Bey, judged that the appropriate medication to prescribe for him was a little dose of whiskey before each meal. Knowing my father's stand with respect to anything alcoholic, there was no way the doctor could treat this as a routine medical prescription, and he also wanted to be honest enough not to hide the nature of what he was prescribing behind some illegible Latin name. Fearful of what kind of response the recommendation of the whiskey might elicit from my father, the doctor first went into a consultation on the weighty decision with my mother. Between them they decided it was at least worth trying. Quite to the surprise of both of them my father mellowly agreed, but on one condition, that it would be the doctor who made the periodic trips to the local liquor store to purchase the stuff. After a lifetime of vociferous battling against drinking, there was no way my father was going to be seen entering a liquor store to make a purchase, even if its purpose was medicinal. This kind of step was at all thinkable only if we assume that, in his early eighties, my father had mellowed in many ways. That he had is further indicated by the fact that in answer to the direct question whether he liked the whiskey, he, with his typical twinkle, admitted that it tasted pretty good.

In general, it is probably true that pacifism, or the moral reformer's instincts generally, no matter what particular cause they may espouse, will have difficulty finding credibility among any who stand outside them. What can add to their credibility is the presence of a certain very basic assumption which my father at least had made. I am not sure that the same assumptions would undergird pacifism or moral reforming in general, but they were certainly there for my father. The first assumption was of course that the world needed reforming, and the less amenable it seemed to be to reformation the more desperately it stood in need of reforming. The world needed to be freed from war (and from some other evils) but the need to be reformed was greatly intensified by the discovery that reform came hard. There may not have been anything very novel about this part of my father's assumptions. But on the question of how reform is to come about he was, I think, fairly unique even among pacifists. Reform could come about only by the radical commitment, or the perfect purity of heart, of the individual person. My father was by habit and instinct in no sense an organization man, and that meant that he never seriously looked to pacifist associations as proper agencies through which to work gradually toward the achievement of an ideal, He would have been ready to make an exception for the Quakers who come to mind first at mention of the "peace churches." This exception would be made for the valid reason that the Quakers were, before they were, in the sense in which they were, organized activists for peace, the pure in heart on the peace issue, with a rare genius for fostering purity of heart. My father did carry on correspondence with individuals within organized peace movements, but such correspondence had little to do with the planning of strategies for peace such as one expects from organized advocates of anything. In fact the few letters from correspondents which I have been able to turn up are in a way not very uplifting, and this is reinforced by recollections of oral comments about various purportedly peace-loving individuals. The letters seemed to dwell on the issue of who among the peacemakers were the really committed ones, and the tone of those comments comes close to sounding oddly conspiratorial. It was not hard to find people who were ready to make anti-war noises, but almost none of these was trusted to be truly committed. And not a little bit of my father's oral effort went into expressions of dismay that there was only such a pitiful little handful of the truly elect.

Even more certainly than that he did not become involved in the organized peace movements outside the political establishment, my father had strictly no confidence that governmental action would sometime change. He was convinced, as pacifists ordinarily are, that government was too irretrievably at the mercy of those who had vested interests in war. Yet he was equally convinced that peace would some day come and that the swords would be beaten into plowshares; but in that he also was confident that this would be wrought less by some eschatological divine intervention than by the peace commitments of the pure in heart.

In this setting he gathered into his consciousness a kind of stable of specially admired people on the national and world scene, who together add up to a pretty unusual assortment. Somewhat surprisingly these are not confined to the sweetly and gently pure in heart. Those he admired were social radicals, though in some instances he clearly did not admire them for what they believed in or strove for but for how they believed and strove. There was, for one example, the famous Carrie A. Nation. I do remember having some difficulty reconciling the image of that terrifying lady with the hatchet with the image of the non-violent pacifist, especially during my more impressionable days when I had fixed on the notion that the hatchet was used on persons rather than on wine kegs and that the red that flowed through the gutters was blood, not wine. Being a person of a not inconsiderable though outwardly controlled temper himself, my father may have found a satisfaction in admiring that tempestuous lady. Much more surprising was the fact that my father spoke glowingly of Samuel Gompers, one of the great figures in the early years of the labor movement in America. His admirations were certainly highly selective and generalized, because, as his later-expressed criticism of the movement toward unionization of the farmers in the depression days shows, he saw no good coming out of the orga-

Pacifism

nization of labor. So Gompers had to be on his saints' list not for what he advocated but for the uncompromising rigor of his advocacy and for his refusal to acquiesce in the existing social status quo. But if he could say nice things about Gompers in spite of his advocacy of a revolutionary new order, he could more easily be a devotee of Leo Tolstoi, partly for his attitudes on war and partly for his instinct for reform by way of maintaining the older virtues of a people that lived close to elemental nature. In that mood, he also throve on Thoreau long before Thoreau became the gospel for a new generation of anti-establishment youth. Lincoln occupied a place of honor in the pantheon, partly because of his sheer humanitarianism but even more for his famous words, in speaking of the institution of slavery, "If I ever get a chance to hit that thing, I'll hit it hard!" which conveniently overlooked Lincoln's time of temporizing on the slavery issue while giving priority to the political aspects of national unity over the moral issue of abolition. William Lloyd Garrison, the fiery abolitionist, was very much my father's kind of person, and his style almost certainly made a major impression on my father. My father saw many analogies between the abolitionist and pacifist movements, and the fact that in time slavery was indeed abolished provided a basis for the hope that in like manner war could be. But towering high above even all of these admired ones there stood the figure of Mahatma Gandhi, "the wizened little pest in diapers," as some scorner put the description. Moderating the fact that Gandhi accomplished what he did through what were after all the raw political forces of the Congress Party in India, for which he provided a focus and a hope by no more or less mysterious means than by articulating its ideal and embodying its hope, my father gave enormous weight to the other part of the image: one tiny individual ranged single-handedly but in a radical moral commitment against the whole weight of the then still mighty British empire and winning.

The inclusion of each of these in my father's heroes' list is credible. That he was also an admirer of, of all people, Napoleon, is hardly so. I have to believe that what made Napoleon appealing was the fact that he was physically of about the same height as my father and gave him some reassurance that even people of short stature need not be impeded from great achievements so long as they have the will to accomplish. In a similar vein, he liked the picture of Alexander the Great sitting down to cry, after his conquests, because there were no more worlds to conquer. It was quite a feat for my father to love that image of the imdomitability of the human spirit and at the same time to hold fast to the belief that the meek shall inherit the earth—to which he also held.

I have said that, as a moral reformer at heart, my father put his trust wholly in the radical purity of heart of the individual as the way by which the world would be changed. Much earlier I indicated that my father also had some problems, not with piety but with the organized church. But these two seemingly unconnected notions now also flow together in his deepest instincts. If he had trouble with the organized church, it was because he saw the church through the lens of the purity-of-heart model—and found it terribly wanting. According to the diary, in those early morning talks with (or *to*) my mother before the rest of the family had begun to stir, a favorite subject of discussion was the failures of the church, and its generally disappointing character.

He looked to the church not for any organized lobbying effort against this or that evil of the times, nor even as the instrument by means of which public opinion might eventually be swung over to effective support of noble causes. If these kinds of items were in his thinking about the church at all, it was clear to him that these roles could never be effectively played unless something else happened first, that the church become itself radically committed against whatever was evil in the world.

As a pacifist, nothing was more burdensome to him than the discovery that the church sounded such a quavering trumpet on the issue of war. Its failure to be uncompromising here was for him no less than a complete abrogation of its sacred charter.

Again, this kind of mind-set is even more concretely evident in his judgment about the church and its attitude toward alcohol. He liked the Methodists, partly for the high quality of John Wesley's evangelism, but probably even more for Methodism's rigorous stand on alocholic beverages. That issue came to a head in a very specific way in the fact that his own church, in the sacrament of holy communion, used fermented wine, rather than the biblical "fruit of the vine," which could as readily have meant unfermented grape juice. To my knowledge my father never took communion in his home church, Old First Reformed in Orange City. On "communion Sundays" he made it a regular practice to attend another church in town which did use the grape juice. And after church on communion Sundays, a favorite topic of conversation between him and my mother, especially during the Prohibition era, was her report to him who among the participants she had been able to observe may have taken an indecently long draught of wine from the large communion cup which in those days was simply passed up and down the long pews. Or they had a field-day together untangling the ingenuities of the Sunday School Superintendent as the time neared for the quarterly "temperance lesson," which had become a fixture in the Sunday School curriculum. One of the responsibilities of the superin-

Pacifism

tendent was to lead the teachers in a discussion of the upcoming lesson at a week-day "teachers' meeting." This superintendent was well known to have been something of an imbiber of spirits, and as regularly as the calendar he always managed to have some "business engagement out of town," at least on the night of the teachers' meetings and often on the following Sunday as well. Those kinds of items do border on the eccentric in the retelling, but they were taken in all earnestness by my father and mother, not for what they amounted to in themselves but for what they pointed toward—a failure of the church's purity of heart, especially on the part of its responsible leadership.

So, in the above sense, as exemplified better than in anything else in his pacifism, my father walked through his times, both self-consciously and by reputation, bearing the image of the radical moral reformer. But that story would not be quite complete without recognition of one final pay-off point. We have some trouble knowing how to cope with the kind of presence he was.

In the main three general options are open to us in our dealing with it. One is the option of ridicule. The lines are not always clear between the genuine reformer and the one whose radical instincts lead him into extremisms which we can ridicule because they border on eccentricity. Even Bertrand Russell, who in later times, along with his performance of intellectual works of sheerest genius, took up the cudgels against war, was not spared ridicule for his efforts to stop bodily certain movements of the military. We do not find it at all hard or uncomfortable to dispose of the eccentric in this way. Or better, we think we do not. We do have some difficulty in knowing whether our acts of ridicule settle the issue or whether they are just a nervous escape from the uneasiness of knowing that the reformer is right and we are wrong. A second option is persecution. Prophets easily fall prey to persecution, on the shaky assumption, I suppose, that if we can but bury the prophets we will also have disposed of what the prophets stand for. But the spirits of the prophets may then rise up to haunt us in the night. The third option is to recognize that the reformers who are driven by the voices of their consciences are also the bearers of our own consciences, to recognize in the short run or eventually that they have been right. If after such recognition there is still struggle on our part, it is only because we cannot bring ourselves to follow the reformers in their reduction of very complex issues to simple black-and-white terms. Or we find it difficult to share their judgment that even our belief that issues are not reducible to absolutist terms of right and wrong constitutes a culpable temporizing with weighty issues of a moral sort, a search for hiding places from what we know in our hearts we ought to be doing.

One of the final crucial questions to ask about a particular reform-minded individual fits into this scheme of options. For on how we answer that depends whether we are dealing with one who has come to embody the reforming instinct at its authentic best. I am not sure whether this question, asked now about my father, is properly answered by me who lived as close to him as I did. My judgment will have to be corrected or confirmed by others.

So far as I can honestly know, my father did not become the object of ridicule for his moral rigorousness which at least bordered on the eccentric. Certainly not overtly. I may myself have been too shielded from what might have gone on behind his back to know for sure. Nor, I think, could it be argued plausibly that he was particularly persecuted. His suspicion that it was because of his pacifism that he was ousted from or kept from this or that desired professional niche may have been well-founded but it may also have been no more than a purely subjective suspicion. If there was any of that, it was I think overshadowed by the other response. He did speak "as one having authority, and not as the scribes," When he spoke people listened. Not only in their later retrospect but at the time, they knew him as a conscience among them and recognized the power of his utterance. It is not hard, in a way, to take stands or to stick with commitments to unpopular causes. It is a much rarer act to retain widespread respect while doing so. And this, I think, my father did achieve.

How, after all, is one to account for the fact that one of my seminary colleagues, by then a mature and self-possessed and quite flamboyant person nearing thirty, who had never before met my father but knew him only by reputation—why did he, when he saw my father coming down the street, quickly stuff his lighted cigarette into his coat pocket, burning a whole so large that it ruined that new and hard-won coat? Why did old Dr. De Bey, certainly no weakling, in appearance or reality, but a big and blunt and confident doctor, wilt at the prospect of having to prescribe a spoonful of whiskey at meal times for my father's heart ailment? Why did those who literally raved against the treason and the sacrilege of pacifism stand mute in my father's presence, or come back later to acknowledge how right he had been? If I knew the answer to that, I would know one of the most important and elusive things about him.

IX
The Editor's Chair

In 1928, my father assumed his new position as the editor of the weekly newspaper, *De Volksvriend*. He was to occupy that position until the spring of 1934, and then to return to it for two years in 1949 at the age of 79. By then he had acquired some status as one of the community's elder statesmen. His products in those last years as editor are hard to distinguish from the earlier ones in any way. They show the same flair in writing, the same intense interest in the affairs of the world, the same ability to see dangers implicit in current trends when no one else seemed able to see them. It has to be some kind of special tribute to him—to his ability to keep himself intellectually alive and to discipline himself against the diminution of his faculties—that he was able to bridge a gap of fifteen years between his first and second stints on the paper without any lessening of vigor or acuteness. And to have been able to do that while he lacked the overt stimulus that comes from having a specific professional role to play in the meantime makes this especially remarkable.

I am sure that acting as an editor is something he had never envisioned himself doing, so intent had he been on the academic life as his instinctive goal and the religious vocation as that into which his circumstances led him. But once in it, though I have no direct word from him on this, it had to be that he found in it a natural outlet for his many-sided intellectual interests and his interest in the common life. A certain routineness of central interest does, after all, characterize the academic life, and that life always runs the risk of becoming ivory-towered. Besides, in the editorship, he could fall into what I think was a natural habitat for him, that of reflection in the isolation of the editor's office. Besides that, working in the immediate physical environment of the sound and sight of linotypes and printing presses and the smell of printer's ink could both reflect and stimulate his consciousness of the power of the printed word, which was a large item in his native creed. He could also build his editorship on a long-standing interest in providing in one way or another the cement that would continue to hold the Dutch people of the middle west together and heighten their ethnic consciousness. By this, he dreamed that the Dutch influence on American culture would become much larger than it ever had been and could reasonably be expected to be.

It will be hard for anyone who has never been close to an editor's role in turning out a weekly newspaper to have or acquire any accurate sense of its proportions. In that kind of context the editor certainly does not preside over a team of functionaries to whom various specific tasks can be delegated, while all he has to do each week is turn out a few paragraphs that will appear specifically as the editorial of the week. It is hard for anyone not involved in the actual writing to have any appreciation even for how long a single newspaper column of print actually is. And if it is generally true that such an editor takes on a labor whose physical proportions are hard to appreciate, my father could be expected, in his passion for doing his job better than he was asked to or than anyone else could, to increase its dimensions well beyond even its average.

I have no way of knowing just who devised his job-description, he or his publisher. If the publisher did, he was a Simon Legree of the first order; if my father did, the publisher got himself a huge bargain, at a hundred or so dollars a month. My father's weekly schedule called for an editorial, of course. In my father's case that called for sometimes a single editorial which filled up to two full columns of newsprint and sometimes two or three editorials in something like that space. Even the task of deciding each week what the subject of the editorial should be had to be taxing enough, though once my father knew what he was going to write about the writing seemed to flow quite freely, and even more freely as he settled into a weekly routine.

Besides the editorials there frequently appeared other articles which loosely approximated what any other paper might call a feature article. These also came from my father's pen, and served as the kind of outlet that permitted him to pursue some interests that he did not judge to fall within the proper purview of editorials. It would be cutting things too finely to try to make any distinction between the intellectual content of these articles and what appears in the editorials, so I shall not try to keep these separate.

But the editorials were only a beginning of that weekly task. Second only to that in importance and in its demands for originality was a lengthy exposition of the weekly Sunday School lesson. The newspaper was not in any sense a churchly publication. It was purely a private commercial venture which had to make its way financially by income from subscriptions and advertising. Since its readership was loosely scattered throughout the upper middle west and the only advertising it could hope to pull in was by local business establishments, it was a constant battle to sell advertising. Even so its publisher gave the image of being a reasonably successful business man. He obviously treated it wholly as a business and without much sense of newspaper mission. But it is a relevant commentary on the readership that an exposition of the Sunday School lesson could find a natural and prominent place in its pages. To that community religious concerns were as natural a part of what made up the fabric of the "real world" as political and economic concerns were. This was a nice boon for my father, for it gave him an opportunity to carry over into his new position his well-developed interest and competence in biblical interpretation, besides providing him with some convenient camouflaging contexts in which he could subtly advocate his convictions on many things. That the vehicle was the standardized weekly Sunday School lesson gave him an added advantage of not having to scrounge around each week for what would for that week be the focus of the reflection. This weekly assignment kept alive for him his instincts for biblical reflection for which over the years his more sporadic outlet had been the sermon.

And then there was the news itself. Local news was quite selectively included, and the selections appear to have been made not so much on the basis of our conventional canons of newsworthiness but on the basis of their "significance"—did the event have any meaning beyond simply the fact that it might have been interesting to know that it did happen? With that freedom to be selective, even the local news-items were more than just reportorial in character, they were triggers, often, for reflections on their ramifications which might lead far afield.

The foreign and national news was not something the paper could simply pull ready-made from the wire or press services. So far as I know it subscribed to no such services, and even if it had the news items would have to be translated. The sources on which my father relied for the news pieces he had to write made some sense but they were also makeshift. His main reliance, a bit incredibly to us who have been made aware of the extent to which that was a quite artificial product, was on the *Congressional Record*. That had the economic advantage of being free, and I am sure the local congressman felt flattered to think that at least one of his constituents was interested enough in congressional doings to ask that a copy of the *Record* be sent. And to rely on that did make some sense. For a very great deal of national news is indeed made in Washington and by Congress, and in the *Record* one supposedly has his access to the considerations that prompted the Congress to take the actions it did take. But to turn the *Congressional Record* into all the news that is fit to print was a Herculean task. Even to identify amid the morass of stuff that appears there items that have news potential is no simple matter, and several of the family were engaged in the task of producing at least a rough reader's guide to what each issue contained. This was done not always as a chore but with some scholarly pride; the record of the acts and proceedings of the Congress comes certainly much closer to being the "raw" history that scholars pride themselves in seeking out than does what would appear in the press services. The paper also subscribed to the *Des Moines Register*, but I do not know what use my father made of that.

As for foreign news, the reliance was mainly on the major Dutch daily newspaper from Amsterdam, *De Telegraaf*. To turn to it as a source also made considerable sense, for that made available to the American readers a European perspective on world affairs, even on American affairs. But the news was, by the time it appeared in my father's paper, pretty old news, since the paper was sent out by surface mail. The answer to that, of course, was that if after two weeks an event is no longer news then it really is not such earth-shaking news to begin with. The real newsworthy events would endure as news much longer than that. This is not to say that my father would fill up his news columns by lifting sections out of *De Telegraaf*; if that happened proper credit was given. Reliance on that source also freed my father, I would guess, from legal liability for plagiarizing the news services—although he probably never thought of that, and copyright laws were at the time a rather loose assemblage anyway.

Interestingly, and surprisingly for one who was himself a newspaperman, there was in our home a ban on daily newspapers, generally unannounced but simply understood to be there. I have no clear idea as to what may have prompted this, whether reading a daily newspaper was judged to take too much time from more worthwhile enterprises, or whether this represented some kind of distrust of the press-media. I simply do not know. The same kind of ban existed against the radio, although we did manage to circumvent that. One of us managed somehow to get hold of a cast-off little portable radio, and it was to the accompaniment of that that we spent our endless hours hand-setting the type for printing my father's stuff; he may have been surprised that at times we seemed as eager as we were to be down in the basement printing room setting type, when in fact we may have been down there because there was something on the radio that we did not want to miss. But by that we were surreptitiously introduced to the finer world of culture: major-league baseball, I think Amos 'n Andy, et cetera. But when footsteps approached off went the radio even if we were in the midst of a great rally in the last half of the ninth inning.

The Editor's Chair

Besides all of that, there was in the weekly paper the "correspondentie." The readership of *De Volksvriend* was, of course, the Dutch-speaking people, who had experienced their own version of the *Diaspora*. And from many of those scattered, mostly tiny Dutch communities there came periodically little collections of local news items. Each community had its regularly designated correspondent (in exchange for a free subscription to the paper, which was worth a couple of dollars a year to the correspondent). The reporting could not have been on a weekly basis; the paper would have been swamped. And no such community could produce three cents worth of news items every week. Even so most of the items concerned such weighty matters as that such and such a family had had dinner on such and such a day with dear old Aunt Tillie. But before we become too uppity about that, we must remember that, at least in my father's judgment, his newspaper could fill the role of holding the Dutch people together as an ethnic identity. That role was significantly fulfilled by the periodic appearance in the paper of names from the different communities. Even I read all of these regularly and thus built up some sense of who lived where and even of what kinds of communities the different communities were. But even these pages of local news items from everywhere had to be edited by my father; even in these he was not about to tolerate bad grammar.

And then there were my father's poems. Every week he wrote a poem for publication in the paper. In fact, Tuesday was poem-writing day. He developed a fairly uniform format for these, though they covered a wide variety of themes. Some were written with an eye to particular events that happened in the community, some were of a much more general character, but they were all long on substance. They were obviously not meant to be just style but a message. This, I would guess, was the only period in his life when he wrote poetry by the calendar, but poetry-writing certainly was not new for him. In his earlier years in South Dakota he had been a quite prolific poetry writer. I am not enough of a literary critic to do much of an analysis of his poetic style. Even I can detect, however, that his poetry provided a fluent outlet for his powerful sense of seeing associations among ideas which would seem at first glance to be quite disparate in character. The result is that many of his poems contain something of a surprise twist. As ingenious as his poems were, his titling of them, and also his associating of each with a relevant biblical quotation, seems to me to have been even more so. Many poems were obviously born out of an imaginative reflection on the meaning of a single word, mostly from a foreign or classical language, with Hebrew terms proving to be more fertile than those from any other language. All in all, each poem carried a heavy message and could be a challenge to intensive reflection. Poetry, I think, may have come more naturally to him than prose, if by prose we mean language especially intended to introduce facts or to marshall rationally persuasive arguments. He was more at home with a "picture-making" kind of reflection and expression, the kind that would be immediately persuasive or not at all. During the six years of his first stint as editor I do not believe he missed a week in his poetry-writing—and, of course, during those six years he never took a week off for vacation. In that time he would thus have accumulated over three hundred poems. Many a poet would surely have envied him that kind of publication outlet. That supply of poems would stand him in good stead during the years after his connection with the newspaper had been terminated. For then, because he was cut off, at the age of sixty-three, from any other viable way of earning a living, he turned to the only thing available to him. He proceeded, on his own printing press, to reproduce those poems as bound volumes and then travelled the country from Michigan and Indiana to southern California and the state of Washington (and I believe there was a trip to New Jersey), to sell his poems wherever he could find a cluster of Dutch people. And he boasted, probably with good justification, that this might have been a phenomenon unique at least in modern cultural history—of a poet writing the poems, physically printing them on his own presses (of course, by way of his sons) and then delivering them directly door-to-door to the consuming public.

One other little assignment fell to his lot as editor, and it says something about his religious disposition to say that this was probably the most distasteful part of his whole task. Prior to his coming to the paper, it had developed a tradition of printing at least some contributed articles. Some of this was of pretty good quality, particularly when it had to do with some aspect of the history of the Dutch people in this country. He did not mind editing and printing that. But the chances were much greater that anyone who thought he had writing talent would write on some religious topic, and within that the chances were very high that that would turn out to be simply a flow of pious chatter. This he had little patience with, but could not escape publishing it, after editing, since the publisher judged that for political reasons he could not turn his back on the "stable" of writers that had developed.

It would surely be most natural to look to all of these outputs as the major source of information about my father's intellectual product, if for no other reason than that these are pretty voluminous when compared to anything or everything else he put out as original stuff. The other item in this original intellectual output consists of three or four formal lectures delivered at various times during his post-editorial years. In

The Editor's Chair

these he carried through the general theme of "a moral interpretation of. . . ." That deserves separate comment later on.

It is hard to know how to go about reporting on the substance of the editorials. If nothing else, the sheer bulk of them gets in the way. Over a total of eight years as editor, there would be over four hundred issues of the paper. More often than not there was not just one editorial per paper but two and often three, so the total swells much beyond four hundred, which means that an enormous range of topics received attention. To keep up with a newspaper's regimen, one must have been able to store up great reservoirs of reflection and possess a facile pen. Having to write to meet weekly deadlines he could not indulge in the luxury of spending long hours brooding over what topic to write about or how to develop a point. It is little wonder that he frequently confides to his diary that he feels very drained. Yet the fact that an editorial was due by a particular hour each week, plus his customary compulsion never to miss a beat on anything he undertook, conspired to keep him going. Taken altogether this constitutes, quantitatively, a pretty impressive output. Though the penmanship began to drag, the quality of the language did not; it continues to scintillate even under these writing conditions. The power to communicate, orally and in writing, the discovery of which in college days had been a factor in steering him into the ministry, had to be his strong point throughout his life. But to have something to say is more than half the battle in communication.

So far as he could know, or I can know, the editorials were widely read. I have tried to read them not from my perspective as an academician but as they must have come through to an average working man's mind. He had developed by now a high standard in which intelligibility and significance were the high points. He did not have to talk down to his readers. At his best he could dip into the highest lore of our cultural, literary and reflective heritage and pull in challenging ideas which tied in neatly with some concrete situational point he wished to make. One could read him without any feeling that he was speaking condescendingly to minds less perceptive than his own, and equally without any sense that one was being pulled out of his own world to be transported into an alien one, as the academic community so easily does.

In trying to pull all of that together, one cannot hope to demonstrate that all of the items find a place in some grandiose pre-conceived intellectual design. His writing on his kind of schedule had to be by instinct more than by preconception or design; and if there are continuities at all they are the consequences of a steadiness in the instincts.

Having said that much, I must also confess that, having relied in anticipation heavily on what I expected to find in the editorials for chapter and verse confirmations of the image of my father which I have from personal recollection and the recollections of others who remember him, a reading of the editorials *en masse* at this late date proves to be a bit disillusioning. I do not think that can mean that I have been mistaken in the image that I have held of him. That was not guesswork. There were simply too many avenues (table "lectures," a letter a week from the time I first left home for college until the week he died, and much, much more) by which all of that came through, and too clear a direct recollection of the fervor and cohesiveness of his convictions to have made that a mistaken image. One cannot decide things like this with complete certainty, but I have to judge now that in so far as his role as self-consciously a man with an editor's responsibility is concerned, he adapted himself reasonably closely to the conventional image of a small-town weekly newspaper editor. Again, what he developed as his major convictions in life came as a result of patient brooding over long periods of time; he could not bring this to his weekly editorials. Time simply would not allow it. The range of subjects with which the editorials deal suggests that he had some kind of resource to which he was exposed from which suggestions for what to deal with came.

If we had just the editorials to go by, in fact, there would be relatively little that would set my father apart from a pretty run-of-the-mill weekly newspaper editor, feeling the need to make some comment about many things. Not only that, but so far as the selection of topics and the manner of the treatment of them is concerned, he comes through very much as a creature of his times, sharing his community's traditional biases, without much show of what I referred to earlier, his ability to come up with better justifications for such shared beliefs than were in the mind of the community itself. True, they do bear his personal stamp. He does not write simply to fill up space. Items that receive his attention do so only because they are connectable in some way with the enormous variety of general or particular beliefs he had come to hold.

But I have to give some image of the editorials themselves. What I opted to do with them was to take a box into which the clipped out editorials were carelessly dumped, mixed them up some more, then simply grabbed a fistful of them and produced the following list of theses. I guess the following would thus qualify as a fair, because purely random, sampling of them. I do not mean to treat the items casually. I only want to say of them that it seems to me that the ideas expressed are in the main simply the articulation of the existing community mores

The Editor's Chair

(for better or worse) rather than showing his character as any kind of prophetic voice speaking to the community.

1. The first quotes at length and with approval a recent article by the warden of a state prison which points out that people turn to crime because of their failure to maintain their religiousness and because of the decline of old-fashioned home discipline.

2. The second is a general complaint against the waste of time and in particular against the waste of time by women who spend too much time at afternoon card parties—even in staid old Sioux County!

3. He argues in favor of requiring allied nations of World War I to pay back to the United States the debts they incurred during the war, since debts are debts and by definition must be repaid.

4. He protests against nepotism on the part of Congressmen with special reference to Senator Brookhart who has managed to get virtually his whole family onto the federal payroll.

5. He worries about the possibility of some secret deal between Roosevelt and Maxim Litvinoff of the Soviet Union.

6. He urges that more careful analysis be made of what, if anything, political speeches really say.

7. He urges that people keep calm by avoiding expectations of dramatic changes and by greater reliance on the steady long-range order in things.

8. He expresses horror at the thought of 50,000 traffic fatalities on United States highways in the year 1932.

9. He worries over the possibility that relaxation of tensions between Russia and the United States as a result of Roosevelt's initiatives will mean an influx into the United States of stronger atheistic impulses.

10. He marvels anew at the wonder of the cow, the horse, the pig, and the sheep as the basis of agriculture and the source of an astonishing variety of things to eat and wear (I do not know what happened here to the chicken).

11. He is dismayed at the contradiction of the churches' lauding the Prince of Peace and yet being opposed to pacifism.

12. He praises a recent lecturer for insisting that Christianity does not concern itself merely with some remote past or future but is relevant to the here and now.

13. He cheers a Texas schoolboard for refusing to hire teachers who will not foreswear dancing, which is opposed not on moral grounds but on the pragmatic grounds that participation in dancing simply leaves teachers too tired to teach effectively the next day.

14. He pleads for support of a recent Senate proposal to establish some world judicatory to handle international differences.

15. He recommends that we pay less attention than we do to politics, which is after all an artificial cultural construction, and to turn back to what is simple and natural.

16. He praises a local choral group for its recent performance of Handel's *Messiah*.

17. He praises the common pine tree and its products, including some kind of natural pine rub which Marlene Dietrich used to relieve her aching muscles after a too vigorous performance.

18. He warns against farmers' working toward a resolution of their problems by trying to define "reasonable price," which there is no way of defining, arguing that the very talk about prices generates a discontent and destroys the joys of farming. Farmers should farm for the joy of it and not be always asking what they can get out of it for themselves.

19. He urges expansion of the export market for farm output rather than paying farmers subsidies for idling acreages.

20. He deplores the fact that while some of our great universities like Yale and Columbia began as Christian enterprises, they have now become purely secularized institutions.

21. He deplores the loss of our power any longer to feel shame, as evidenced by the development of a nudist colony near Allegan, Michigan.

22. He attacks a proposal to legalize liquor for the sake of the revenue this can provide for the state.

23. He happily reports that an English aviatrix, one Lady Hay, world-famous for the smoothness of her skin, credits this wholly to the fact that she gets plenty of sleep at night.

24. He deplores the growing drift toward leniency on the part of juries.

25. He deplores the governmental policy which encourages the perpetuation of tribal American Indian customs and religious beliefs, while going all out for welfare relief for the Indians.

Now, I surely do not find this at all uninteresting. It reveals that he was pretty much aware of what was then going on in the world, including governmental policy on Indian affairs and Marlene Dietrich. Maybe editors expect too much of themselves when they think they have to make judgments on literally every kind of thing that happens. But at least that is preferable to treating everything that happens with casual indifference—if indeed we who are not editors do that. Maybe we do not. The chances are better, I think, that we do indeed react with our own value-judgments to the events we read about; then what is special about editors is that value-judgments are articulated, and that they have the courage to hold them up for public scrutiny, which most of us might not. Nor can a sampling of this kind be faulted for the extent to which it includes references to seemingly trivial matters, rather than moving forever on the purportedly loftier plane of general principles. Maybe it is healthier to recognize that life does consist not so much in our being manipulated by or manipulating principles as it does in our being affected by particular and often seemingly trivial incidents. If some of what appears in the sampling of items seems *passe* (and I am not sure that on a more careful reading they would be justifiably read as being *passe*) then it is probably because they reflect the mores of a half-century ago, and mores do keep changing. But is that fact a discredit to them? Would a similar articulation of current mores look all that much more elevating than those old ones? Are our own "solid virtues" more solid than the "solid virtues" to which my father in his time makes a more or less overt appeal? Considerations of this kind make me wonder about my first impulse to look at these and suppose they represent a relative mediocrity in my father's output.

If any lack appears, it then consists in something else. It is our inability to see the kind of major coherence, of interest and principle, which we wish to find when examining a person's literary output. And along with that, in this random sampling one would not be aware of the intensity and fervor with which my father was committed to major guiding principles. Nor could we understand such commitments because we could not, and maybe even he could not, see how principles are intertwined. It is not clear that the principles, such as they are, have any central focus. So in the further comment, I want to move toward some greater coherence. Obviously it would be too artificial to tie up everything my father thought about everything into one neat little package. But it is possible and important to try this with at least one block of his editorial interest. That is his addresses to the farmers as farmers. For this I rely only in part on the scattered references in the editorials; I have to supplement that with recollections of his oral expressions and other written matters.

He does seem to have operated self-consciously on two tracks in his editorializing. One of these is his address specifically to the problems of farming itself. These editorials are uniformly and explicitly addressed to the farmers. "Aan den Heer Agricola" (to Mr. Farmer) is his salutation for them. The other track includes everything else, though in these he wrote no less self-consciously with his farm-folk constituency in mind. This much of the structuring is his own. The closer structuring of his thoughts on the farmers' life is mine.

In his address to the farmers he knew better than to presume to tell the farmers how to handle the mechanics of production and selling which farming is about, though he probably could have told them something about even this. He was always the inquiring student as far as the mechanics of farming was concerned. What he does address himself to is what we should call "the philosophy of farming," the set of assumptions, political, economic, social, or ethical, within which the enterprise was to be carried on. He was probably more perceptive than most people are to the fact that these assumptions are not merely givens. With respect to these some options are open, and he was simply forthright in arguing for one set of options rather than another. Or, in a closely related sense, he recognized that in course of time these assumptions changed under the pressures of circumstances. Yet those changes were not always simply forced on the farmers by circumstances over which they had no control; they were as much the consequences of what the farmer wanted and thought of as being in his own interest.

In this context my father certainly was not disposed simply to echo the farmers' thinking. On the contrary, he put up a stiff resistance to the changes he saw taking place, and he warned the farmers of the long-term consequences of the policies they were vigorously pursuing. Most of these, he saw, were taking place as a result of the farmers' interests (in which they were certainly no different from the rest of us) in getting more return for less effort. And probably the most basic challenge he offered to this was his preaching to the farmers about the dignity and the joys of work. He knew this would somewhere strike a responsive chord. For though the farmer and his family did put in long hours of physical toil, the fact of the matter was that for one who had grown up on the farm the expenditure of physical energy, even a lot of it, was far less a bane than it was satisfying. It was, as my father knew from his own experience, not in pain that a farmer threw his bone-weary body on the bed at night but with a feeling of real satisfaction. Besides, a farmer's work was so varied, over a year and even over a month or a day, that it was never boring. Nor was the output of energy unceasing. Even the busiest days of the year, the August harvest times, offered gaps for rest and sociality. For my father, the real source of complaint at the strenuousness of the farmers' labor was the wish to emulate the shorter hours of the factory worker or the white collar class. To him to measure life in terms of how little one could get by with doing was a wholly artificial valuation.

He argued against acceptance of coming trends on other grounds than just the appeal to the dignity of hard work. The wish to get more for less effort was asserting itself prominently in three emerging developments. One was the growing mechanization of agriculture, another was the tendency to turn to the federal government for support, and the other was the movement toward unionization of the farmers. He staunchly resisted each of these.

He warned the farmers against yielding to the appeal of mechanization. And mechanization *was* appealing. It made sense for the farmer that he would be able to avoid having to spend the time he spent readying his four or six or eight horse spans before the day's work could even begin. It made sense to use the feed that went into providing his horsepower rather to increase the amount of product he could market. My father simply could not understand, however, the mentality of one who would trade in the joys of working with horses for having to work long days in the monotonous din of a noisy tractor while breathing in its foul exhaust fumes. On these aesthetic grounds "horse power-farming" was much more appealing than the mechanization toward which the farmers were moving. In this he was influenced by his honest love for living things, especially horses. Years later, after the second world war and its aftermath during which there had appeared an international convention outlawing genocide, he, with I think a straight face, was ready to promote a similar code against the "genocide" of horses.

But economically the move toward farm mechanization made even less sense. For him part of the genius of the farm operated by horsepower was that the farm's power source was able to reproduce itself. He agreed to promote mechanization whenever someone would produce a tractor which could beget baby tractors. And with a perspicuity that could not have envisioned the explosion of energy costs in the seventies, he warned the farmers that they were headed for a time when they would owe their souls to the Standard Oil Company (and now OPEC), a foreboding which today's energy costs vindicates with a vengeance. One cannot avoid musing whether not only today's farmer but the country's economy as a whole would be better or worse off had the farming community been willing to heed my father's warnings. I have talked to some reasonably successful farmers who drool at the thought of operating today a quarter or half-section farm with horse-power—freed from the killing burdens of today's enormous costs in energy and equipment.

The move toward relying on the federal government for help, first mainly by market regulations by the manipulation of tariffs, later by more or less direct subsidy, and still later by production control and Henry Wallace's proposal to slaughter little pigs (which had something of the same effect on my father as the Herodian slaughter of the innocents)—this move roused my father to a spirited antagonism, to put it mildly. It was hard to produce a convincing counterweight to the drift, however, difficult to convince the farmers that they were really selling their birthright as a free people for a mess of instant pottage. This was not, after all, a matter of having something taken away from them by an enemy, nor even a matter of their losing something precious through inattentiveness; it was what the farmers thought they wanted and considered to be in their own self-interest, while for my father it was a matter of sacrificing a long-term interest for a short-term gain. But in that context his drawing an analogy between the Communist development and the local situation, on the ground that both were undermining the farmers' independence, remained unconvincing even to these staunchly anti-communist people. He expressed his dismay that the only thing that registered with them was, as is common to evangelicals, the fact that Communism was atheistic. What was atheistic was to them a demonic negation of what they believed but they were so intent on regarding Communism on this level that they could not understand my father's insistence that the Communist damage to the quality of life was what they ought really to be worrying about. Nor could they follow my father's argument that when people began to rely on what lay outside them in pursuit of their self-interests, they were doomed eventually to fall victim to what they relied on. And Henry Wallace's policies of ever-increasing regimentation of production were to him the eventual concrete proof of this.

The third disaster that the farmers were inviting into their lives was the increasing move toward unionization. There was nothing particularly new in the fact that the farmers were organized, and my father had no trouble with that in itself. No one was a more enthusiastic admirer than he of the great things the farmers had accomplished by the development of their various marketing cooperatives. And I suppose there is only a fine line between this and the new thing that frightened him. It was the farmers' recourse in the tough days of the depressed thirties to the more brutal tactics of power which had become increasingly the weapon of the urban industrial unions, specifically the weapon of the strike. Those were by no means easy days for him. It is a mark of how large was his identification with the farmer's life that, though he was not given to worrying about "the last days," he laboured under the powerful foreboding that his world was coming to an end. And he felt a keen sense of identity with the Old Testament prophets who, though in very different circumstances, warned of a coming doom, but were voices crying in the wilderness because no one listened. By my not wholly confident recollection, the force of the depression was by a few years slower in being felt in rural America than in the urban centers, but it did hit hard when mortgage foreclosures on farm properties began. The gloom deepened when the incredible dust storms began, and the South Dakota which he had not ceased to identify with began to blow eastward, and Iowans had to live day after demoralizing day through the near darkness of the pitiless life in the dust. This had all the force for him of a biblical plague, as did the equally incredible devastations by grasshoppers. In all of this my father truly wept with them that wept, and I can still see him daily and pitifully scanning the sky for some of the signs of coming rain which he had learned to read so well.

But all of this could not shield him from an equally intense anxiety over how the farmers were responding and what long-range damage this would do to what had been the historic grandeur of the farmer's lifestyle. When farmers, even his friends, armed themselves with pitchforks and barricaded the highways forcing the tank-trucks loaded with milk to dump their cargo into the ditches in a move to force up milk prices, it hit him very hard. Or when angry farmers invaded a court-room and carried the federal judge out onto a country road and stopped just short of lynching him just fifteen miles from where we lived (even though it happened across the line in Plymouth County and God stopped at the outgoing boundaries of Sioux) he joylessly saw all his unheeded warnings vindicated.

In all of this stance against what the farmers were doing to their future, he was the kind of person who would quickly be written off as a reactionary. But in all of this he saw himself as the almost isolated guardian of the grand values of agrarian America. And this judgment was not merely an emotional reluctance to leave a past behind him—a past which he indeed did feel strongly attached to even though it had not been particularly kind to him. He was able to see past the hardships to the romance of living in rural America. But his was more than just a kind of aesthetic judgment. It was equally, as he saw it, a pragmatic judgment, though a long-range one. By that judgment, farming would not, by so much as the farmer went in for mechanization for which there were no foreseeable limits, remain a viable venture. But beyond this, he measured everything from the perspective of his original Frisian disposition to which I referred earlier, the disposition to remain free and unencumbered in the exact sense of resisting anything that put the individual at the mercy of circumstances beyond himself, in so far as that was possible, but especially resisting anything that put him at the mercy of other people. This came as close as anything I could name to being the absolute in terms of which he carried on his own affairs, and it was also the perspective from which he measured the processes which he saw developing outside him. And he read with growing dismay the annual farm census figures which showed all too clearly how rapidly America was moving away from her agrarian character.

It was not that he was opposed to the processes of industrialization per se. He was not so dense as to imagine that the world could or would or should stand still. But if industrialization should come he hoped, all too vainly, that it would take a particular shape. He read of Mahatma Ganhi's plea for the development of village industries in India, and became enamoured of the possibilities for that in America. This is simple for us to dispose of, on the ground that never having lived in or even near a large city, he was simply biased against urban life by his own experience. And when we look at that village-industry proposal in the light of the enormous and seemingly inevitable drive toward urbanization, it seems analogous to a person's standing on the shores of the ocean crying out to stay the movement of the tides. Were he to take note now of how mind-boggling the urbanization process has become, with the once largest city, New York, now paling in comparison with Mexico City or Tokyo, and see the horrors of urban blight and hear today's talk about how the cities have simply become ungovernable and how life in the city has become impossible for millions, while also observing the flight to the suburbs and industry's flight to the hinterlands—though he was not given to this, he might in that setting have yielded to the temptation to say, "I told you so."

But his days as editor also came to an end, a premature end, as everything else had, and again not by his choice or because he saw a larger opportunity in something else. Here there was no alternative to which he could turn. The paper was obviously not his. He would by now, so great had he become involved in his career as editor, have given his right arm to have been able to take over the ownership of it. But he had no financial resources with which to do so, nor did he possess the courage or ingenuity to seek financing of it, though I have no doubt that had he done so he could have gained this, such was his standing in the community and his reputation as a successful editor. And I think he could have managed the operation of the enterprise, since he had for those six years closely observed all the facets of the operation. Maybe he simply did not possess the kind of self-image which would have led him to think of himself in that capacity. He saw himself at best as an employee, not as a potential employer.

I do not know just what did lead to the termination of his services as editor. I do not even know whether it was a matter of his resignation or of being let go. The image we received of all of this at the time did include the fact of growing friction between him and his publisher, and

I suppose it did not make much difference whether he resigned or was fired. In either case, his integrity, his freedom to write from his convictions was at stake. The editor had taken on another employee who, my father was convinced, was there as a spy.

The differences between him and his publisher were, so far as I can know, differences in editorial policy. And that seemed to consist mainly in a political difference. These were the beginnings of the Franklin Roosevelt era. And to my father Roosevelt was unmitigatedly a satanic figure. (The only exception I know was when Harold Ickes, Roosevelt's Secretary of the Interior, came out with a proposal to combat the dust-bowl phenomenon in South Dakota by means of an enormous program for planting rows of trees as wind-breaks on the plains. The theory behind this was that the prairies should never have been broken up by the plow, and that this had happened only by the greed of those who originally did this. Short of letting the land revert to its prairie status, Ickes imagined that the situation could be remedied by such a program for developing windbreaks. So much of an apostle of tree-planting had my father been that anyone who even talked of planting trees had it made, in his estimation.)

Roosevelt had gotten off to a bad start, as far as my father was concerned, by building his first political campaign on a promise of repeal of the Prohibition amendment. Recalling the campaign oratory, it is hard to avoid the feeling that that issue loomed larger even than the desperate economic situation, incredible as that must sound in retrospect, except for the fact that the Repeal issue had come to be the symbol of individual freedom. Against the background of that, nothing that Roosevelt would propose by way of turning the country around from its depression could hope to get a respectful hearing from my father. Hoover with his stubborn reliance on traditional laissez-faire economics became the epitome of everything that was noble and good. His publisher, on the other hand, saw Roosevelt as the hope for the future. He was, in an environment in which the term "liberal" was a dirty word, a member of that part of the community which, not without a trace of superciliousness, fancied itself to be liberal.

But a sampling at least of what my father was writing in those days in his editorials does not seem to warrant any image of possible radical clash over anything. Many of the editorials, though articulating a general pattern of old-fashionedness, seem harmless enough and hardly the kind of thing that could lead to a sharp rupture between editor and publisher.

I have to suspect, therefore, that beneath the surface there was a basic difference not so much of editorial policy as of temperament, and that the differences of a political sort provided the publisher with a reasonably graceful exit from a relationship which never had been enthusiastic. I have to write the following with some diffidence because I never got to know the publisher very clearly as a person. He was basically an aloof person, as I remember him. He also identified himself with the more sophisticated society of the community, and I do not find it hard to imagine that he found my father a somewhat uncomfortable person to have around. Part of that was because of the vigor with which he wrote and advocated his positions in the community. But part of it may also have been simply that he was not the kind of person who would add any glamour to the business. He did nothing to burnish his general public image, and even rather fostered the image of a slavish drudge in the performance of his task. Whatever the reason, the productive and rather enjoyable term as editor did come to an end.

X
The Man on a Bicycle

This time no alternative position did turn up. It was, after all, the depth of the depression, and at best positions of any kind moved with frustrating slowness. And my father was now sixty-three years old, and even in those years long before people thought of sixty-five as the normal time for retiring, his age was against his being gainfully employed at anything, especially in the areas of his interest, education and the church. And we must add to that the fact that one who had for so long been identified with something other than the parish would no longer even be thought of as a potential candidate for a church position. Fortunately for him, he did have his acreage to fall back on, so was always in a better position than any of the urban unemployed during the depression. He could at least stay alive with an amazingly small amount of cash outlay for anything. There was also the small printing establishment set up in a room in the basement at home, and in one way or another a dribble of job-printing came his way, mainly because his prices were so delightfully low. There were also frequent opportunities to serve as a guest minister in churches, locally and in the larger community in which he had become a familiar figure during his missionary days in Dakota. Some of this involved spending three days, a Saturday to make train connections to get there, and a return on Monday, possibly catching some fitful sleep on the hard benches of some railroad station as he waited through the night for his train connections—all with a net cash reward, after expenses, of five dollars, if he was lucky.

But at least one thing was open to him to do which he could do without having to wait for anyone else to open the doors to him. He took to printing his past and current writing in such a form that he could go out to sell it door to door. But to do that he also had to acquire some kind of mobility. A car was out of the question, if not financially then temperamentally. For the immediate area he could manage with his trusty horse and buggy, and up to a point he did. But if the venture were to become viable at all he would have to greatly enlarge his domain. So his eye fell on the bicycle as a means of conveyance. This would give him a rather ideal mobility, since a bicycle would be easily transportable from town to town in a railway baggage car. Once at a destination he would be able to maneuver freely and with reasonably good use of his time. He could hardly hope to make a go of his venture if he opted to remain within the confines of the towns. Too many of the people who were his prospective customers were scattered out in the countryside. And with the bicycle he could carry a small but adequate supply of literary wares with him.

But he first had to learn to ride a bicycle. I surely would pass along this advice to anyone who has any idea of anytime in his life riding a bicycle, that he learn to do this when he is young. That turned out to be some kind of an ordeal, for my father, who at times despaired of ever learning the art, and for us who ran behind him hour after hour of practice to keep him from falling over. But that hurdle, too, was crossed, and for many years the bicycle became his public trademark, and it was by that that many, many people were to remember him. There came a time when to ride a bicycle sixty miles in a day was commonplace and he seemed never to tire, even though the roads were often not paved but gravelled and the terrain, though not exactly mountainous, was not particularly a pancake either.

So the venture gradually got under way, and it, along with the not inconsiderable sustenance he could extract from his fertile little farm, was the main source of his cash flow for I would guess upwards of ten years. My recollection is that it was not unusual for him to come home from a four-or five-day jaunt with a couple hundred dollars in his pocket— but that was, believe me, a well-earned couple of hundred. The effort, both physically and psychologically, was enormous. Food and lodging were apparently never a problem. So well was he known and such was the spirit of natural hospitality among those he called on and such was their receptivity toward someone from outside the community that when he arrived at someone's door at coffee-break or meal-time or at dusk he was (I devoutly hope!) readily received and invited to share what was there or to stay the night.

I have, I confess, some difficulty in imagining anything that would be more out of character for a person of my fathers' temperament than being a door-to-door peddler of anything, or even a stationary salesman of anything. He was not, it is true, averse to trying to influence how people behaved and selling does loosely fall into that class of activities. But it is so direct and so overt, so much a matter of doing something, of parting with some generally hard-earned cash, and the selling had to be done clearly for one's own eventual benefit. There simply was not naturally anything of that in him anywhere. It was true, this was not his first fling at peddling. I cannot recover the exact circumstances in which he had done something like this before; all I remember was that for a couple of summers in South Dakota, mostly, I think, in the latter half of the summer, he had done some door-to-door selling of all sorts of school supplies. I guess this must have been a way of eking out a meager salary while he was doing his second stint at the Academy in Harrison. And before that, during his days as a roving missionary in Dakota, there had been a good deal of going door-to-door, only then it was a matter of bringing whatever people bring who are on a spiritual mission. I suppose the same necessity which is sometimes the mother of invention can also be the mother of rationalizations which can make one feel better about doing sometimes distasteful things. He was, I guess, a salesman with a difference, whose greatest risk was that once perched at a kitchen table over a cup of coffee, he would simply talk his day away. Maybe it was easier to think of oneself bringing poetry and culture than it would have been to think of oneself selling pots and pans or Fuller brushes. Would you ever have imagined what it must be like to have a salesman, often a stranger, come to your door in the midst of the busyness of the day to sell you a book of poetry? But it was not always poetry. Gradually his little collection grew, and as a salesman his pride and joy was that he had had the ingenuity to include among his wares a book of collected jokes, "Wit-bits for Two-bits." With that, he seldom went away from a doorway completely empty-handed. So maybe it would seem too unkind to balk at buying a two-dollar book of poetry; no one after that could resist at least placating the salesman by buying a book of jokes. Let it never be imagined that my father was without a sense of humor—or even of salesmanship, after a fashion.

Only the slightest hints of this sense of humor have been dropped along the way. One might not have expected that on a first meeting, or after having read so much in this account of how he agonized over the direction the world was taking or over the issues which he felt were crucial. He did come through as dour, as never quite having lived down the austerity which he saw in himself by virtue of his birth in November on the shores of the stormy northwest coast of Europe. He also described himself, however, in the autobiographical novel that he wrote, and I think honestly and not merely for literary effect, as being a very witty person and having established that kind of public image for himself. In his speeches and writing and even in his sermons, he repeatedly brightens up the area just behind his words with a subtle little flash of levity. I am not sure just how this sense of humour tied in with everything else he was. It probably did not provide him with the grace not to take himself too seriously, but did provide him with alternating moments of relief from his seriousness. His sense of humour was a natural accompaniment of his genius for seeing analogies between seemingly unrelated phenomena. When these analogies are stretched far enough they do have a way of becoming funny, because then they slip over into the incongruity which is the soul of humor. Nor was this trivial. His humour and wit were legendary among those who got to know him.

The easiest part of his humour to talk about is the obvious love he had for hearing and telling jokes. Sprinkled through the inchoate masses of newspaper clippings that are left among his papers are many such jokes, and that he took the pains to clip them was indication enough that he liked them. Often he came back from the office or a trip bearing some new joke which had to be reported at the family table, and then as funny as the joke were his own irrepressible giggles in the telling of it. The typical joke, I guess, was built on the play between double meanings of words. As might be expected, nothing was risque or even borderline. He was too bashful to risk telling anything that was not clearly not off-colour.

But he had the larger flair for seeing the funny side of actual happenings where no one else would have thought there was one, and is remembered for having sometimes turned tense moments into bearable ones by seeing or inventing such wisps of incongruity. His humourous touch was quite uniquely his, analogously to the way in which the finest distinguishing nuances of meaning in a language are caught only in the idioms of its humour. I cannot avoid the conclusion (or at least the hope) that, on net, he had more genuine inward fun in living than the record may have led us to suspect.

Two things during this period chiefly occupied his attention, other than the production and distribution of his writings. The first was his renewed attention to the study of foreign languages, though it would be misleading to suggest that this interest was ever dormant. He now had more free time to devote to it. He also picked up some spot opportunities to teach formal language courses at the college, among them Dutch. That triggered a plan to produce a beginner's textbook in Dutch, which did not get beyond the notebook stage.

Language, and languages, were as much as anything intellectual a major passion for my father. Language is obviously any intellectual's bread-and-butter tool. My father's interest in language is certainly not surprising, especially since he went through four years of Latin and Greek in high school and considerably more in college and professional school. His graduate study at Yale was a most curious hodge-podge, but it did play up Semitic languages. Other than a short-lived dream of going into mathematics, his academic dreams centered on becoming a professor of languages.

He did write a very brief (two-page) "chronology" of his life shortly before he died, but a quarter of this is devoted to telling about the foreign languages he knew. We went through early life quite awed by the general mythology about his having known fifty-two languages. This is pretty impressive, until you begin to ask questions about what in that case is meant by "knowing" a language, and until you become aware of the extent to which language patterns fall into families of languages—Scandinavian, Slavic, Romance, and the like. One who learns even to the point of moderate competence one language in such a family of languages will, given a little imaginativeness in detecting shifts from one language to another, feel at least a little at home among the other languages of the family—enough, I suppose, to be able to pick up a newspaper in that language and get from it some sense of what it is all about. It had to be in some such sense as that that my father was, in almost hushed tones, describable as "knowing" fifty-two languages.

His own listing of the languages he "knew" is much more modest than that, cutting it down to a fourth of the more glamorous list. Of the dozen or thirteen, four (and I think only four) could be said to have been "known" in the full sense of that term: Dutch, Frisian, English, and German. "Knowing" a language in this sense means an ability to handle the language in all the typical conditions in which we rely on language—in formal speech and writing, informal conversation, and popular and scholarly reading. When such a level of competence is reached, it is no longer a matter of doing one's thinking in one language and then translating it, laboriously or fluently, into another. One then "thinks" (and, as my father pointed out, possibly even dreams) in that language; my father could *think* in Dutch or English or Frisian or German.

The other eight or nine languages which he "knew," he knew essentially not as languages to be spoken but as languages to be read. There were Latin and Greek orations, to be sure, but these were at the time carefully prepared before having to be spoken. Russian he never spoke but did read quite extensively. Quite late in life he did get a notion that he might like to learn to use the Russian language orally. I am not sure whether the Berlitz language program had been invented by that time, but he would not have been able to afford it if it had been. Somehow, I think through a mutual acquaintance, he learned of an elderly Russian lady in Sioux City through whom he was able to work on the pronunciation of the Russian sounds. This may or may not have been at about the same time that he was in touch with a Hebrew rabbi in the same city who was to teach him the arts of the Hebrew chant. He did practice the latter on his family, by way of memorized Hebrew biblical passages at mealtimes, but I do not believe he stuck with that very long.

I am not certain that he would have concurred in this judgment, but it is my recollection that of all the languages with which he had any intensive contact, it was Hebrew that occupied a special place, and he developed a keener sense for it than for the other languages. His forte with respect to Greek and Latin was that he had, and these provided him with, a keen sense of word structure and of the interconnections between words. This sense he developed even more strongly in dealing with the Hebrew. Though I do not know enough about Hebrew to be sure of this, I think his special appreciation for Hebrew was even more penetrating in that there is a rich pictorial meaning in Hebrew which fitted in smoothly with his own sense for poetic imagery. Marshall McLuhan's "the medium is the message" had not yet been invented, but, and in a very different sense, I think my father felt that he "felt" the meanings in the sounds of the Hebrew words. He was interested in and quite adept at eliciting great depths of meanings from a single Hebrew word.

There is a sidelight on this fascination with the Hebrew. When students were finished with their professional training in the seminaries, they were required to appear before the church classes for examination in their qualifications for professional licensure. These examinations included examinations in the two major biblical languages, Greek and Hebrew. It generally fell to my father to serve as the designated examiner in one or both of these, partly because his fellow-clergy, on the average, tended to be shaky in their own linguistic competences, and even if they had the competence they were frightened to betray the level of it in the presence of my father's linguistic reputation. It is, of this I can assure you, wholly a myth conjured up in the frightened minds of generations of students, that in the examination my father expected them to respond in the languages in which they were being examined. But he thought it was reasonable to expect that after their three years of professional study they would be able to sight-translate at least the more familiar and simpler Greek and Hebrew passages. The custom had developed generally for students prior to the examination to agree with the prospective examiner on a specific passage which would be the subject of the examination. These requests for prior information naturally also came to my father, and had the would-be examinees been able to hear my father's privately rendered expressions of disgust at their stupidity and their shortage of scholarly instinct, they would probably not even had dared to show up for the examinations. I think the story was that at least for a time my father never responded

The Man on a Bicycle 145

to those pre-examination requests for an assignment, in which case the students passed anyway, probably as much as anything because of the sympathy of the other clergy. We really knew that my father was mellowing when in later years he did respond to the requests and gave a specific assignment ahead of time.

Naturally my father was as staunch an advocate as there ever was of the study of foreign languages, and he, as such advocates are wont to do, did his share of claiming that virtually supernatural insights could be gained by such study. But his claims were not easy to refute since he stood there as Exhibit A of how enriching the right kind of foreign language study could be. His remaining papers include notebooks and many scraps of paper which reveal how and how much he worked reflectively on word studies, not because he had some particular assignment to which such study might be relevant but simply because his spontaneous interests led him in that direction.

But back for now to the book-selling venture. In that one thing led to another. At first western Iowa, southwestern Minnesota, and southeastern South Dakota had been pretty much the limit of the field of operations. But presently he began to cast covetous eyes toward the more populous and compact Dutch areas in southern Chicago and the Chicago suburban area. He seemed to be much too unaware of the great dangers of making his way by bicycle along the then already busy streets of Chicago, but he did come through unscathed. Once that area was reasonably saturated he looked longingly toward the West, toward the Dutch communities in the state of Washington, and around San Francisco and Los Angeles. This involved, of course, long train rides, but the usual costs of that were cut in half because all railroads in those days extended the courtesy to clergy of letting them travel for half-fare. So he began, so late in his career, to become familiar with many communities which during his years as editor he had come to know only by the sporadic little columns of news notes intended to be published in the paper. The world became much larger than he had ever dreamed it was, and the first look beyond his beloved plains states was not wholly encouraging, He is reported to have muttered, after his first spectacularly scenic trip by rail through the Rockies, "there is an awful lot of wasted land out there." But it all grew on him, and as might be expected, when anything grew on him it also had to be written about. This took the form of yet more books, this time travelogues, of sorts, but still heavily overlaid with the kind of rambling commentary at which he had become adept. There was here and there even some light philosophizing about what he had encountered, all of which was specifically aimed at the mind of the ordinary Dutch folk and calculated to renew their appreciations for their environments and their heritage which, through sheer familiarity, may have begun to seem commonplace to them. And then on the second time around to the west, what Californian could resist buying a book about his own California, written with an eye to his own perspective rather than that of the standardized geography book or travel guide description? This kind of wider-ranging travelling was also tied in with preaching engagements in various Reformed churches on Sundays and later came to be merged also with his special interest in seeking out and bringing some of their own true culture to the scattered Frisian groups. It was particularly by way of both of these ventures that he widened the circle of his acquaintance and became known to a much larger area.

This kind of enterprise was hardly conducive to any sustained intellectual enterprise, nor was there any specific stimulus to call that forth. But in the interstices of time during and between these treks which might cover as much as a month at a time, neither his mind nor his pen were ever long idle. It is to this period, and perhaps a little later, that we owe what I think is his most specific effort to articulate a central perspective from which to think about some major notions, though it had long lain in his instincts.

Except for this brief attempt at producing something that he could identify as his central intellectual focus, his intellectual energies were scattered. Aside from the editor's years, when he wrote in response to current events or trends and little items he ran across in his reading, we have to rely for information on his notebooks. One such notebook, which thus reveals something about the character of his intellectual work-habits, is filled with notes and bits of information, much of it culled from, of all places, the *Congressional Record*, which turned out to have been a more versatile source than one would have expected. For the *Record* did go far beyond simply being a journal of what actually transpired in debate on the floor of Congress. It was a kind of catch-all for everything the members of Congress had said or wished they had said or wanted to say without having an opportunity to say it or wanted their constituencies to think they had said. But the items he thus picked up were filtered very much by his own interests. Another notebook is especially interesting because it is filled with a kind of original reflection which had nothing to do with any of his diverse professional responsibilities. They were brief reflections on philosophical concepts in a narrowly technical sense of "philosophy." They are an explicit indication that he did have an awareness of philosophy in that technical sense.

They show an ability to do a fairly sophisticated job of conceptual analysis—of "time," "object," "matter" and the like. From this I have to infer that though he had had only one formal course in philosophy in his educational career, that one at Yale, that kind of interest stayed with him as an intellectual hobby. In fact, the kind of thing that appears in that notebook is not exactly typical of philosophy early in the century, when philosophers were much given to thinking "sweepingly" and "in the grand manner"; it is more prophetic of what was to become philosophy's later style, that of working toward precision of thought.

But besides this there is also that fling at doing something to articulate what he clearly intended to stand not merely as an occasional lecture but as a central theme in his intellectual make-up. Its content is brief, consisting of a few formal-lecture length essays (which might mean an hour or an hour and a half in the reading). At least two of them were delivered at a Western Seminary convocation in Michigan. The focus was now on attempting a "moral interpretation"—potentially of everything that was there to be given an interpretation of. It gathered up something that had been long a part of his intellectual instinct, at least by so much as the term "moral," in whatever context it might be heard, had acquired a special magic for him—maybe from his early days when he had read the Kantian *Critique of Pure Reason* through in its entirety, in the original German. If anything among his writings can qualify clearly as his very best intellectual effort, this was it. In nothing else that I know of his writings, certainly in English, do all of his reflective and prose talents reach a better exemplification, both in substance and in style.

The first of the lectures is on "A Moral Interpretation of the Universe," bearing also a second title, "A Moral Cosmogony." Though it was originally delivered as a formal lecture forty-six years ago, it would even today make for good listening, since it deals with issues which are not only still timely but which have received, if anything, even greater prominence in the scholarly world since that time. The language is beautiful and "in the grand manner," yet simple and direct. It contains as wide a range of allusions to the major intellects of our heritage as one is likely to find anywhere in so short a space, without in any way raising the feeling that here is merely an encyclopedic assembly of opinions; they bridge the worlds of philosophical and literary articulation: Plato and Kant, Schopenhauer and Berkeley, transcendentalism and Hinduism, Mary Baker Eddy and Einstein, La Place, Darwin, and Tyndall, Sir Isaac Newton, and Euler, these are all there. So are Genesis and St. Paul, Job and the Psalmists, William Cullen Bryant, Wordsworth and Tennyson. Together it is itself a literary work of art of the highest order: one wonders how all of the items and imagery could have found their way into one piece, yet when it is done there is nothing one would point to and say of it that it was redundant to the purposes of the lecture. It deals with something of profound and far-reaching import, yet it is said with a twinkle in the eye without being flippant. As is everywhere his style, there is no argument; if argument is anywhere intended it is wholly as a by-product of a "showing" what may be the case and trusting its intrinsic worth to be persuasive. It is written, as so much of what he wrote was written, self-consciously from within a Christian perspective yet it is not left dependent for its worth on the presence of that Christian idiom; thus he succeeds in employing the Christian idiom to reach beyond itself toward a universal meaning.

At issue is the question of how we are to conceive of our relation to the physical universe; or, in later idiom, what category of thought best captures that relation, which is defined by the nature of what we ourselves are. There is no doubt about where he wants to go with this. That is cued in not by some theory but by his own deepest intuition about his own relation to nature, at least verging on a nature-mysticism, his awed love for everything that lives and moves. But he has no interest, as lesser minds are wont to do, in maintaining this at the expense of other alternatives; he has the larger courage to reach for this without scorning something else. The "moral interpretation" of nature is not to the exclusion of but is a transcending of other conceptions.

The "moral interpretation" is the third in, roughly, an ascending series of conceptions of the relation, the first being the sensuous relation of ordinary and of scientific perception, and the second the conceptual relations which are the scientist's milieu. Even to see a qualitative difference between the world as *per*ceived and scientifically *con*ceived is pretty perceptive for one whose overt educational background was what his was. He has ambiguous feelings about the first of these, not because he cannot make up his mind but because there seems to be no way of avoiding that ambiguity. He has some fears of the impoverishment of our relation to the world which accompanies not merely the perceptual process but the quantification of nature which is the natural accompaniment of perception, and deplores even there the extent to which the formal educational processes are locked in and confined to a quantitative treatment of nature. Yet he pleads with the young seminarians for whom the lecture was intended to lay aside, wholly or at least now and then, their biblical commentaries and give themselves a chance to let nature touch them *perceptually*—there to read of God in the book of God's nature. (Elsewhere he had said, "Nature is God's secretary.") Nor does he have any problems with that other, and qualitatively separate, image of nature given in the scientist's conceptual structuring of it. This disposition is not in any sense merely invented by him to serve the purposes of a particular speech; all his native instincts led him to a deep interest in and positive appreciation for the achievements of the theoretical sciences, an appreciation unmarred then by the welter of anxieties that were to arise only in our time over the damage that could come to nature by our scientific-technological exploitation of it. Though in some of his thinking about things he was inclined to give his own simple and final answers to issues others would only wrestle with, he, no more than we have been able to, did not presume to settle the age-old issue whether the conceptual structures of the sciences were read into or added to nature by us or discovered to be in nature itself, but he was clearly aware of the issue. Beyond these two relations to nature, and in some way created in them even though not inferrable from them, is the "moral" relation. This receives no exact definition, maybe because it inherently defies subsumption in any one of the concrete images we may associate with it. The term "moral" is, again, one of those magic words, for all of us and especially for my father, which is pregnant with an abundance of meanings we cannot hope to grasp all at once. He does reject the appealing alternative terms "spiritual," "religious," and "theological" in favor of the term "moral," which, for a detectable reason, becomes the larger term which embraces the others as they cannot embrace it. It will include the common poetic theme that by looking at nature we encounter God, as in and beyond nature, as the name we can give to interpersonal communion with nature. But it also includes what is rarer in such poetic descriptions, the sense that in our confrontation with nature we are also hit with the sense, not now of our littleness before nature, or of our personal communion with a personalized nature, but of our moral impurity in the presence of nature—exemplified in Tolstoi's account of "a tragic moment, when a wretched seducer of innocence shuddered at the sight of the moon emerging from the dark clouds."

That first venture in "A Moral Interpretation" (of Nature) was followed three years later by a second formal lecture on "A Moral Interpretation of History," also delivered before a seminary audience. Here he moved in a milieu which was clearly and admittedly less familiar gound for his thought than his thought about nature, and he gives indications that he deliberately set out to build a background for this by reading some major works having a bearing on the philosophy of history. He begins by recognizing that the difference between "history" and "nature," difficult though it may be to designate certain events as belonging to history and others to nature, is that nature is a *given* for us, while history is the history of human behavior, with nature being the context in which history occurs. This is an important beginning, inasmuch as it follows from that that we cannot speak as readily of history as something by which we are bound as we can of nature in those terms; or if we are "bound" by history, it is the collective act of mankind by which we are bound. He also is clearly moving in a philosophical orbit by insisting that what he says about history is what one would say about history regardless of its actual specific content. Not surprisingly for a person who has lived his life, as my father did, in a deep sense of the moral, he quotes with approval Admiral Byrd's reflection: "I believe that the age-tested convictions of right and wrong are as much a manifestation of cosmic law and and intelligence as are all other phenomena," and he insists on a tri-partite nature of man, not in the sense that these are compartmentalized into independence of each other but that all of these are essential if we want to give a complete account of the nature of man. But it is not the usual tri-partite distinction which is to be found among Christian thinkers: physical, mental, and spiritual; it is the materal, the mental, and the moral (my father loved such alliterations). He speaks out against a naturalism which wants to reduce man eventually only to the levels of the animal (or chemical) reactions. But if history is man's actions and man is moral, then, neatly, history becomes collective morality. With this he counters Reinhold Niebuhr's thesis, in *Moral Man and Immoral Society*, which he read as meaning that the locus of morality is exclusively in the individual and not in the society, with the insistence that the locus of morality is the society, the sum total of human acts, more than it is the individual. While he is sensitive to some of the implications of this (a corporation's acts cannot be claimed to be properly morally indifferent) it is clear that he failed to see how this was not quite consistent with his own long-standing commitment to the belief that morality may require defiance of the corporate. But in the insistence that history is the collective morality he finds occasion for reaffirming the Kantian moral axiom, "So act that you could wish your action to be a universal maxim,' but also makes clear that that axiom is open to many competing interpretations. Where Kant made such universalizability a test of whether an act is moral, my father turns it (a little uncertainly) into either his favorite thesis, to which I referred earlier, that society will eventually be made over by the purity of the individual heart, or that society, the collective morality, ought to reshape its conduct to conform to the ideals set by the individual conscience. As important as anything else, however, in this whole thesis is the fact that it lays a foundation on which one can construct the belief that society may be held to be accountable to the moral law.

The theme of "moral interpretation" is then extended to include a treatment of two other topics which were dear to his heart. There is "A Moral Interpretation of Memory" and "A Moral Interpretation of Language." I think these were given somewhere also as formal lectures but I cannot locate evidence as to the time and place. If they were, this was either at Northwestern College or at Marion College in Indiana. In extending the idea of "moral interpretation" to include now the two items of memory and languages, the relation between the items and the overall thesis under which they are subsumed inevitably becomes more tenuous. A broad theme like "moral interpretation" must, of course, prove its warrant exactly by its extendability to an ever-widening range of human interests. Such extendability is meant to strengthen it but in the end is more likely to weaken it simply because by making it do more than it can we tend to water it down.

There is an accidental quality about the fact that the theme is now extended, beyond the concepts of nature and history to these two, memory and languages. It simply *happens* that these loomed large in my father's set of attentions, either by the accident of disposition or by an accident of experience. Memory and languages are, in some sense, therefore of less universal intellectual interest than are nature and history.

All his life my father had made much of the act of memorization, from the time when he, on his own, memorized poems and recited them when "company" came to their home in Frisia (and then went around to take up a collection!), to his memorization, in Frisian, of *Enoch Arden*, in his sixties. Beyond that, as I have mentioned, he saw the habit of memorization as uniquely a way of staying aging's process of mental deterioration, and even, in his customary vigorous way of extolling a good thing, as a way of inching along toward immortality. His final achievement, on the evening of the night he died, was to recite from memory for my mother a chapter of the Bible which he had been struggling for a few days to master.

Little wonder then that an undertaking under the title of "A Moral Interpretation of Memory" turns out to be an essay in praise of memory, in a style not very different from Emerson's, except that the allusions may be richer and more varied. It is hard to know why this should be called a *moral* interpretation, unless that bears the connotation that memorizing is something we ought to pay more attention to, or something it would be profitable to work harder at. But if that is present, memorization is still not offered as a duty we should perform. It is made compelling simply by showing to what extent, and mainly without our realizing it, the power to memorize is a necessary condition for attaining some other things, like knowing or reasoning, which we prize as our fundamental and distinguishing human characteristics. If memorization is thus extolled as a nice ideal, it is also accompanied with reassurances that it is something that can be done and can always be done better; he even gives some pointed hints as to how it can be done better.

If in dealing with memory, the phrase "a moral interpretation" tends to drift off into more of a personal trademark than an illuminating characterization, in speaking of language, there is at least a move to make the label say something. "Moral" is equated here with "spiritual," but that not in any conventional religious meaning of that term; it is opposed to "a mere material or mechanical concept of language." But this, too, starts out in the direction of simply magnifying our images of language, in one statement, typical of how my father's mind worked, pointing out that "civilization is the product of the composition of these two forces, fire and speech." (Or, in speaking of oral language: "God gave us a mouth for the two important functions of eating and speaking.") It accomplishes this magnification of language simply and effectively by dwelling now on this obvious aspect and then that one, in the total picture which language offers. His special cues are drawn equally and harmoniously from the French scholar Ernest Renan's famous old classic on the origin of language and what the Bible says about language. He sees in the former interesting confirmations of some of the things said in the latter. And it all concludes with two perorations. The first of these brings him around to what had been a major passion of his career, the dream that by learning to understand each other's languages we might learn to understand each other, and by understanding each other usher in the kingdom of the Prince of Peace. The second may stand as an expression, in his twilight years, of how he had understood the content of his life's intellectual commitments, or at least how he wished in retrospect he might have gone about them: "to speak the truth in love." Of his commitment to the truth and his commitment to other persons and their well-being there can be no doubt. These two together make up an epitaph by which he would be proud to be remembered.

Such was our "heit," as Frisians proudly speak of their sires. Twenty five years after his death, his death in contentment after an often stormy life of struggle, sometimes against difficult circumstances and sometimes against the disappointment that the world has been so slow to live up to its own best visions of what it could be—I say, twenty-five years after his death, the use of the past tense seems strangely out of place. Such *is* our "heit" sounds very much more appropriate. Above everything else the knowledge of his contentment in his commitment and the sense of his presence remain very real.

"Belief in immortality" certainly carries connotations which we may never be able to exhaust. But somewhere among the hundreds of cues which point toward its meaning there must be room for this, that he is very much alive in the vivid sense of his presence among us to whom he gave so much.